SHELTON STATE COMMUNI
COLLEGE
JUNIOR COLLEGE DIVISION
LIBRARY

DISCARDED

W9-BZG-797

18.00
209
P.

HD   Dobb, Maurice Herbert, 1900-
4909
.D6   Wages
1982

DATE DUE			
JUL 2 3 1996			
SEP 16 1996			
OCT 1 6 2013			
Nov 19,2014			

WAGES

THE CAMBRIDGE ECONOMIC HANDBOOKS

General Editors

J. M. KEYNES (Lord Keynes)	1922–1936
D. H. ROBERTSON (Sir Dennis Robertson)	1936–1946
C. W. GUILLEBAUD	1946–1956
C. W. GUILLEBAUD ⎫ MILTON FRIEDMAN ⎭	1956–

HD
4909
.D6
1982

WAGES

MAURICE DOBB
Fellow and Lecturer of Trinity College, Cambridge
Reader in Economics, Cambridge University

DISCARDED

GREENWOOD PRESS, PUBLISHERS
WESTPORT, CONNECTICUT

Library of Congress Cataloging in Publication Data

Dobb, Maurice Herbert, 1900–
    Wages.

    Reprint. Originally published: London : Nisbet ;
Cambridge : University Press, 1928. (Cambridge
economic handbooks)
    Includes index.
    1. Wages. I. Title. II. Series: Cambridge economic
handbooks.
HD4909.D6 1982   331.2   82-994
ISBN 0-313-23483-3 (lib. bdg.)   AACR2

All Rights Reserved.

First published 1928.
Reprinted with Revisions 1959.

Reprinted with the permission of James Nisbet & Co. Ltd.

Reprinted in 1982 by Greenwood Press,
A division of Congressional Information Service, Inc.
88 Post Road West, Westport, Connecticut 06881

Printed in the United States of America

10 9 8 7 6 5 4 3 2 1

INTRODUCTION

TO THE CAMBRIDGE ECONOMIC HANDBOOKS
BY THE GENERAL EDITORS

SOON after the war of 1914–18 there seemed to be a place for a series of short introductory handbooks, " intended to convey to the ordinary reader and to the uninitiated student some conception of the general principles of thought which economists now apply to economic problems."

This Series was planned and edited by the late Lord Keynes under the title " Cambridge Economic Handbooks " and he wrote for it a General Editorial Introduction of which the words quoted above formed part. In 1936 Keynes handed over the editorship of the Series to the late Sir Dennis Robertson, who held it till 1946, when he was succeeded by Mr. C. W. Guillebaud.

It was symptomatic of the changes which had been taking place in the inter-war period in the development of economics, changes associated in a considerable measure with the work and influence of Keynes himself, that within a few years the text of part of the Editorial Introduction should have needed revision. In its original version the last paragraph of the Introduction ran as follows :

" Even on matters of principle there is not yet a complete unanimity of opinion amongst professional economists. Generally speaking, the writers of these volumes believe themselves to be orthodox members of the Cambridge School of Economics. At any rate, most of their ideas about the subject, and even their prejudices, are traceable to the contact they have enjoyed with the writings and lectures of the two economists who have chiefly influenced

Cambridge thought for the past fifty years, Dr. Marshall and Professor Pigou."

Keynes later amended this concluding paragraph to read :

" Even on matters of principle there is not yet a complete unanimity of opinion amongst professional students of the subject. Immediately after the war (of 1914–18) daily economic events were of such a startling character as to divert attention from theoretical complexities. But today, economic science has recovered its wind. Traditional treatments and traditional solutions are being questioned, improved and revised. In the end this activity of research should clear up controversy. But for the moment controversy and doubt are increased. The writers of this Series must apologize to the general reader and to the beginner if many parts of their subject have not yet reached to a degree of certainty and lucidity which would make them easy and straightforward reading."

Many though by no means all the controversies which Keynes had in mind when he penned these words have since been resolved. The new ideas and new criticisms, which then seemed to threaten to overturn the old orthodoxy, have, in the outcome, been absorbed within it and have served rather to strengthen and deepen it, by adding needed modifications and changing emphasis, and by introducing an altered and on the whole more precise terminology. The undergrowth which for a time concealed that main stream of economic thought to which Keynes referred in his initial comment and to which he contributed so greatly has by now been largely cleared away so that there is again a large measure of agreement among economists of all countries on the fundamental theoretical aspects of their subject.

This agreement on economic analysis is accompanied by wide divergence of views on questions of economic policy. These reflect both different estimates of the quantitative

importance of one or another of the conflicting forces involved
in any prediction about the consequences of a policy measure
and different value judgments about the desirability of the
predicted outcome. It still remains as true today as it was
when Keynes wrote that—to quote once more from his
Introduction :

> " The Theory of Economics does not furnish a body of
> settled conclusions immediately applicable to policy. It
> is a method rather than a doctrine, an apparatus of the
> mind, a technique of thinking, which helps its possessor to
> draw correct conclusions."

This method, while in one sense eternally the same, is in
another ever changing. It is continually being applied to
new problems raised by the continual shifts in policy views.
This is reflected in the wide range of topics covered by the
Cambridge Economic Handbooks already published, and in
the continual emergence of new topics demanding coverage.
Such a series as this should accordingly itself be a living entity,
growing and adapting to the changing interests of the times,
rather than a fixed number of essays on a set plan.

The wide welcome given to the Series has amply justified
the judgment of its founder. Apart from its circulation in
the British Empire, it has been published from the start in the
United States of America, and translations of the principal
volumes have appeared in a number of foreign languages.

The present change to joint Anglo-American editorship is
designed to increase still further the usefulness of the Series
by expanding the range of potential topics, authors and readers
alike. It will succeed in its aim if it enables us to bring to a
wide audience on both sides of the Atlantic lucid explanations
and significant applications of " that technique of thinking "
which is the hallmark of economics as a science.

C. W. GUILLEBAUD
MILTON FRIEDMAN

April 1957

NOTE TO THE FOURTH REVISED EDITION

REVISIONS in the present edition have been confined to those necessary to meet the passage of time. These are mainly to be found in Chapters II and III, and consist of supplementary information (together with some deletions), covering the period of the last ten years. There are also a few small alterations or additions in the last two chapters.

In the Note that prefaced the Third Revised Edition of 1946 the author indicated that, while " large parts of Chapter II have been rewritten ", " the most drastic change, as a result of reconstruction and rewriting both in 1938 and to-day, has been in Chapters IV and V concerning the theory of wages : chapters which retain only a little of their original design ". In the present edition these theoretical chapters remain substantially as they were left in 1946. A further major reconstruction of them seemed out of the question ; and to patch their deficiencies seemed likely to make them more rather than less unwieldy. Accordingly, for good reason or ill, they have been left as they are.

M. H. D.

Cambridge,
OCTOBER, 1955.

CONTENTS

CHAPTER I

THE WAGE-SYSTEM

PAGE

§ 1. Introductory 1
§ 2. Slave, Serf, and Artisan 2
§ 3. The Characteristics of a Wage-System . . . 4
§ 4. Economic Freedom 5
§ 5. The Growth of a Proletariat 9
§ 6. Different Degrees of Dependence 11
§ 7. Wages and Net Product 13

CHAPTER II

WAGES AND THE STANDARD OF LIFE

§ 1. Distinctions and Definitions 16
§ 2. Wages as a Proportion of Total Income . . . 18
§ 3. Money Wages and Real Wages 23
§ 4. Wage-rates and Earnings 27
§ 5. Index Numbers of the Cost of Living . . . 32
§ 6. Movements in Real Wages 39
§ 7. Poverty 44

CHAPTER III

THE PAYMENT OF WAGES

§ 1. Wages and Cost of Production 50
§ 2. Wage-payment and Incentive 54

PAGE

§ 3. Piece-rates and " Speed-up " 55
§ 4. Rate-cutting 58
§ 5. Premium-Bonus Systems 60
§ 6. " Task-Bonus Systems " 62
§ 7. The Bedaux System 63
§ 8. The Field of Payment by Results 66
§ 9. Sub-contracting 70
§ 10. Weighing and Measuring. 72
§ 11. Truck and Deductions 74
§ 12. Profit-sharing 75
§ 13. Payment by Results and Earnings 77
§ 14. Sliding-scales 81
§ 15. Hours of Work 85

CHAPTER IV

THEORIES OF WAGES

§ 1. What a Theory of Wages tries to do . . . 88
§ 2. Traditional Theories of Wages 90
§ 3. The Subsistence Theory 91
§ 4. The Influence of Habit and Custom . . . 93
§ 5. Marx and the Power of Collective Bargaining . . 96
§ 6. The Wages-Fund Doctrine 98
§ 7. The Theory of Marginal Productivity . . . 103
§ 8. Marshall and Supply and Demand 107
§ 9. The Supply of Labour 110
§ 10. Inventions and Wages 112

CHAPTER V

WAGES AND BARGAINING-POWER

§ 1. The " Laissez-faire " View 118
§ 2. The " Normal " Competitive Wage 120
§ 3. Two Qualifications 123
§ 4. Standards of Consumption and Investment . . 126
§ 5. Imperfect Competition in the Labour Market . . 128

PAGE

§ 6. The Influence of Monopoly and of Excess Capacity 130
§ 7. How Far can Wages be Raised ? 133

CHAPTER VI

WAGE DIFFERENCES

§ 1. Differences between Grades 138
§ 2. " Non-competing Groups " 141
§ 3. Differences between Industries and Districts . . 144
§ 4. " Casual " Employment 146
§ 5. The " Sweated Trades " 147
§ 6. Men's and Women's Wages 149
§ 7. " Equal Pay for Equal Work " 154
§ 8. International Wage-differences 155

CHAPTER VII

TRADE UNIONISM AND WAGES

§ 1. The Character of Trade Unions 160
§ 2. The Beginnings of Trade Unionism 161
§ 3. The " Old Unionism " 162
§ 4. The " New Unionism " 165
§ 5. Trade Unions and the State 168
§ 6. Reformist v. Revolutionary Trade Unionism . . 170
§ 7. Workers' Control 171
§ 8. The Machinery of Collective Bargaining . . . 176
§ 9. Conciliation and Arbitration 177

CHAPTER VIII

THE STATE AND WAGES

§ 1. State Intervention 180
§ 2. The Wages Council System 181

PAGE
§ 3. Minimum Wage Problems   186
§ 4. State Arbitration   189
§ 5. The Future of Wage Policy   191

      Index   195

WAGES

CHAPTER I

THE WAGE-SYSTEM

§ 1. Introductory. There has been a good deal of discussion among economists as to how universal economic principles can be held to be : whether they can be held to apply to any type of economic system (so long as it is based on some form of exchange) or to be particular to a certain set of conditions and social institutions. Economists have been frequently taunted with their love of Robinson Crusoe analogies—with their tendency to generalize from some simple economic society to the complex world of to-day, in disregard for the various institutions which separate the modern world from Crusoe's. But whatever view one may hold of the wider question, there will be few to deny that in dealing with the wages question one is dealing with something that is very intimately related to the conditions of our modern economic system, and that the problems which one meets derive their essential shape from the special features and institutions of that system : for example, from the form in which property is owned and its distribution and from the nature of production and the division of labour.

To the discussion of wage-problems, at least, Robinson Crusoe analogies and the search for " universal principles " seem to be of little use. They may even be misleading in distracting our attention from features of the problem which we should see to be of prime importance if our gaze were focused more realistically upon conditions as they actually are. To start by studying the *differences* which distinguish the present-day setting of our problem from the past seems to be the most promising means of disclosing what is important, as well as an essential preliminary to appreciating correctly such true similarities as exist. If we examine the features which distinguish wages as they are paid to-day from other ways in which work in times past was performed and paid for, and seek to define the character of the present wage-system in these terms, we shall see that some fundamental distinctions exist which give a unique character to the actual problems with which the modern industrial system is faced.

§ 2. **Slave, Serf and Artisan.** There are three systems in the past with which the modern wage-system may be contrasted and compared.

First of these, there was Slavery, under which the person of the worker was owned by his master and could be bought and sold. The whole time of the slave was at his master's disposal; and the master fed the worker as much as he thought fit to keep him in working efficiency, and made use of the slave's working time either to minister directly to his needs and fancies or for commercial purposes to produce a product. The master's income depended upon the number of slaves and upon the extent to which the product of their work exceeded their subsistence : their subsistence represented his cost or outlay, and what they produced above this his surplus or " net revenue ". When the supply of new slaves was plentiful and slaves as a result were cheap to buy, the master did not need to spend much on keeping them, and he could afford to work them hard and exhaust them early and then replenish his stock by buying slaves anew. When, with the cessation of new conquests or the decline of the slave trade, new slaves became more scarce and more costly, then a

slave as a more valuable object required to be more circum-
spectly cared for : probably the master had then to provide
enough for each slave to breed and rear a family as well.

Secondly, there was Serfdom, which prevailed over most
of Europe in the Middle Ages under feudalism, and has
existed in slightly different forms at other times in various
parts of the world. Here each village was mainly self-sufficing,
and trade outside the village-unit was the exception rather
than the rule. The serf did not belong in person to a master,
but owed certain services by customary right to his lord, and
was attached to the lord's estate and could not move from it.
Often he was bartered with the estate, as in seventeenth- and
eighteenth-century Germany and nineteenth-century Russia
estates worth so many " souls " were mortgaged or purchased,
and as Edward I in England made a grant of royal mines
to his Italian creditors, the Frescobaldi, together with the
compulsory labour of the " King's miners ". Usually the
serf procured his subsistence by working certain strips of land
which he held as his own by customary right, in return for
the obligation to devote the remainder of his time to cultivat-
ing his lord's fields or working in his lord's household. The
land held by the serfs and the time that was their own had to
suffice to maintain themselves and their families. The more
fertile the land and the more productive the labour the smaller
this area of land and this time needed to be, and the larger
was the surplus which the lord could command from the
surplus labour of his serfs. The value of an estate depended
on the size of this surplus, as the capital value of a slave
tended to depend (if the slave supply was limited) on the
surplus arising from the employment of a slave.

Thirdly, there is the free craftsman or artisan working with
his own tools in his own workshop and marketing his own
products, or in agriculture the independent peasant farmer
working his own holding by the labour of himself and his

family. It is a system of which we find examples in nearly all ages, alike in classical times, in the towns of the late Middle Ages and at the present day. Here the worker is, in a sense, his own employer, making and selling his own product, and retaining for himself any surplus or " net revenue " above the cost of his own materials and his own subsistence.

§ 3. The Characteristics of a Wage-System. If we compare these three systems with one another and with the modern wage-system, it will be clear that an important respect in which they differ is in the differing degree of economic freedom enjoyed by the worker, this in turn depending on the relationship in which he stands to economic property—either owning it, or not owning it, or himself being regarded as property in the possession of a master. It is the form which property-rights take which determines the form of relationship between men—between social groups or classes. Under both slavery and serfdom the freedom of the worker is closely circumscribed by law : under slavery he is entirely subject to a master, and under serfdom his freedom is strictly narrowed by his obligation to perform specified service for a lord. But under the wage-system the worker is bound by no such legal ties. Before the law he is his own master, free to work or not as he pleases, free to hire himself for wages, or to work as an independent artisan if he prefers. The capitalist who owns a workshop or a factory or a farm, since he can no longer command any compulsory labour, either by traditional right or by purchase, has to hire the disposal of a labourer's time for a day or a week, paying for the hire a market price, and securing his profit out of the difference between the wage he has to pay and the price he gets for the finished product which he sells. Hence, the removal of all legal restrictions on the labourer's freedom is usually found in history as one of the prior conditions for the rise of a wage-system.

§ 4. Economic Freedom. Here the classical economists of a hundred years ago were usually content to leave the matter, stressing the freedom of the wage-system as against the compulsory systems which had gone before. This system attained the maximum of freedom that was possible in this deterministic world : it was as free as the system of the independent artisan, while being more efficient. True, the wage-earner bound himself to work certain hours in a factory under the discipline of the employer's overseer, to take orders and obey, whereas the artisan was his own master and worked in his own time and in his own way. But in doing so the wage-earner consented of his own will by free contract : his will was free to decline the terms of employment if the proffered wage was not fair recompense for the unpleasantness of what he undertook. Wages were a fair price in a free market for work done, just as was profit an economic price to the employer for the services he performed ; and the fact that some chose one means of livelihood and some the other was only a special case of the general division of labour which brought such increase to the wealth of nations.

This view, however, is not the whole of the matter, and on examination turns out to be so one-sided a picture as to contrast in some respects grotesquely with reality. One can, of course, imagine a system of equal and unbiased opportunities (which it implied) where the majority of persons faced the choice at some stage of their career between working for a neighbour or setting up as an employer on their own. Something approaching it is probably found in a peasant village, or was found in the early mediæval town. But there is little resemblance between this idyllic picture and the society of to-day. In the actual wage-system of modern industrial civilization the choice of the labourer has in fact been much more drastically curtailed. The limitation of choice, it is true, is no longer a legal limitation as of old ; it is an economic limitation which is as effective of its kind as the legal compulsions which it has supplanted. This limitation consists in the fact that, in the conditions of modern capitalism, the labourer is a member of a propertyless class : a fact which narrows his freedom of choice and confines it to those means of livelihood which do not require the possession of any land or capital—or even in the majority of cases any considerable education or training. In other words, it confines his choice, as a rule, save for a few fortunate " Dick Whittingtons ", to hiring out the labour of his hands for a wage. In every case in history where a wage-system has appeared, the rise of this system seems to have been preceded by the appearance of a class of persons without the means to set up as independent artisans or peasants, or else by a considerable narrowing of the sphere within which craftsmen of small capital themselves could operate at a profit.

It may, of course, be argued that such a narrowing of opportunities does not of itself constitute a restraint upon the labourer's freedom in any significant sense. Man is never free to do anything he pleases : Nature always imposes a ban, and herself circumscribes his choice. Alternative opportunities cannot be measured, and often cannot be directly compared as between different persons or between one age and another. The " free and noble savage " had in many ways fewer opportunities than the modern wage-earner, and the peasant of Eastern Europe or of China than the Ford-employee of Detroit. What sense can one make of such comparisons if one includes under the term " freedom " so vague a collection of things as the term " economic opportunity " represents ?

While freedom is not something which can be quantitively measured, something is undoubtedly meant by the term which can be compared as being greater or less. Moreover, it would clearly be artificial to limit the term solely to *legal* limitations on a person's actions, when so many other external limitations, particularly of an economic or social character, exist. But to arrange things in a series or order in such a way as to make a comparison of " greater or less ", it is necessary that what are compared should have a close resemblance in all other respects than that in which they are being compared. It may not be possible to compare the " freedom " of people to-day and several centuries ago in any sense which does not include the sum total of their economic welfare. But it is perfectly possible in any given age or society to compare one class of persons with another with regard to the opportunities in which they differ, taking for granted the benefits (or burdens) which are common to all society. In the case of the modern wage-earner, the special limitation on his freedom with which we are concerned is his inability to gain a livelihood except by concluding a contract of employment with those who have the land or capital to set him to work. It is certainly possible to compare his position, in respect of the freedom it affords, with that of his employers as a class ; which is the important point for our purpose. His employers have less urgency (since they possess property) to conclude a bargain with him than he has to conclude it with them [1] : they can become wage-earners, if that should seem more profitable, and can probably gain access to other occupations from which he is debarred by lack of means ; whereas he can hardly cross over and become an employer himself, save by rarest good fortune or in some purely hole-and-corner way of business. Hence, the labourer, because of his smaller economic freedom—his more circumscribed choice—is dependent on the capitalist to a greater degree and in a more significant sense than the

---

[1] In technical language this can be expressed by saying that the two constitute " non-competing groups " in the main, to one of which the marginal utility of income is much greater than to the other. This difference will determine the terms on which they are willing to trade.

capitalist is on him : a fact which will clearly have a fundamental influence on the wage-contract between the two.

Such a dependence, economic and no longer legal in
character, will be a dependence, not of a labourer on one
particular employer, but of labourers in general on the whole
class of employers or potential employers. At the same time
this will be reflected in the particular character of the relations
between workmen and any particular master. This dependence is apparently so universal a characteristic of a developed
wage-system on a large scale as to justify one in treating it as
one of the defining characteristics of such a system. At any
rate, it is evidently a characteristic of the wage-system under
modern industrial capitalism.

This is not to deny that the performance of work for a
wage might be found in cases even when no such dependent
class existed. There might well be cases where many persons
found it more attractive to work for another than to work on
their own, even at a wage-level which left a considerable
surplus to go as profit to their employer. This situation could
be the result of very wide differences in the natural ability
or in the enterprise and initiative of different persons to
organize and manage production and so to make a business
of their own a success. But it seems very unlikely that
differences in innate ability alone would ever be so great as
to give rise to such a widespread and obstinate preference for
wage-working that the system extended to all lines of production and became the predominant mode of production in
each trade. One would hardly expect the system to embrace
all industry and to become universal in this way, still less to
reach the point where there were hundreds and thousands of
workers to each employer, unless differences of economic
advantages and opportunity between different social groups
had developed as well. There is certainly no evidence that the
historical development of the modern wage-system was the

outcome, in the main, of anything of this kind. On the contrary, one seems to find the relationship of wage-labourer and master becoming a universal feature of the industrial system as the result of a prior development of important social differences between classes—social differences involving differences in economic opportunity—of which differences in property-ownership are the chief.

§ 5. The Growth of a Proletariat. One can, accordingly, say that to the rise of a fully-matured wage-system two things are necessary. First, the removal of legal restrictions which bind the worker to a particular master. Secondly, the growth of a propertyless class, or a proletariat, willing to hire itself for wages because it has no alternative livelihood. Without the first development the worker remains a serf or a slave, and not a wage-earner selling his labour in an open market. Without the second it will hardly be profitable for employers in general to organize production on any considerable scale on a basis of wage-labour. In this country the former change occurred comparatively early, when the custom spread in the fifteenth century of allowing the serf to " commute " his feudal services for a money payment or a rent for the land he held. In other countries it did not come until later, as in Germany between 1806 and 1812, when a series of laws in different States abolished serfdom, and, latest of all the large European countries, in Russia in 1861 with the decree on the emancipation of the serfs.

The second development occurred in a greater variety of ways. Partly it occurred through the natural growth of population, in excess of the numbers that could be accommodated on the land ; and existing land, becoming scarce in relation to the demand for it, acquired a considerable value in the hands of its owners and grew to be only obtainable at a price. The process was accelerated by the enclosure of land which had formerly been held or used by the small peasant-holder in customary right, and the transfer of the land into the hands of the large landowner. This occurred in England in the series of enclosures to facilitate sheep farming which created the race of " sturdy beggars " of which we hear so much in Tudor times, and by the series of Enclosure Acts between 1750 and 1850, devised to encourage modern methods of arable cultivation. In Germany (in contrast to Denmark) similar enclosure of land on a large scale took place at the time of the emancipation of the serfs, as compensation to landlords for the loss of their feudal services. A similar effect is produced in certain parts of Africa to-day by the reduction of the natives' tribal reserves or by the levying of hut or poll taxes on the native when he lives in the tribal reserve and does not work for wages outside.

At the same time in the towns the gilds, both of master-craftsmen and of traders, were becoming increasingly exclusive by a double process of obtaining charters which made it illegal for any other than a gild member to carry on that particular calling as a master, and at the same time of restricting entry into the gild by severe entrance fees and qualifications and apprenticeship regulations. By the sixteenth century in England the larger part of the wholesale and export trade of the country was a close monopoly of a comparatively small circle of wealthy traders, while at the bottom of the towns there existed a growing class of labourers having only a limited possibility of gaining access to any of the craft gilds and of setting up as master-craftsmen on their own. A partial reaction against this tightening monopoly occurred in the seventeenth century, when men of capital began to give out work to be done by small craftsmen in the villages under what came to be called the Domestic System, thereby avoiding the close regulations of the town craft gilds. Any man who had sufficient capital to buy a house and a loom or a knitting-frame could set up as a craftsman in the countryside. But these country craftsmen themselves tended to be dependent rather than independent—dependent on the "merchant manufacturers", as they were called, who gave out work to them to do, as West End tailoring houses give out work to-day to be done as home-work or in small tailoring workshops. Usually the domestic craftsman, being a man of small capital, could not undertake the marketing of his wares himself or conduct anything but quite a small workshop. Often he had the raw material advanced to him by the "merchant manufacturer", who collected the finished product from him in due course and paid him a price for the work done. In certain cases the craftsmen even rented their tools from the capitalist who employed them, as in frame-knitting where they rented their frames. As time went on many of them came to live more and more on credit advanced by the capitalist, and to be in debt to him, and so to be tied exclusively to one employer, as appears to have been common in the hand-tool trade. In other words, many of these craftsmen came to be virtually employed wage-earners, just as in peasant countries it is common (unless special institutions exist to prevent it) to find a propertyless class developing as a result of the progressive impoverishment of a section of the peasantry by indebtedness and the mortgaging of their land to traders and moneylenders. As a final stage in the process came power-machinery and factory production, which by competition took away the livelihood of the hand-loom weaver or hand-toolmaker, and forced all except those who had the means to set up a factory themselves to migrate to the towns and seek wage-employment.

§ 6. **Different Degrees of Dependence.** Inside the wage-system itself, however, the economic freedom of the worker can vary fairly widely. On the one hand, where the workers

possess strong trade union organizations having large funds,
or where they have built up prosperous co-operative organizations from which they have special facilities for securing their
food supplies or for obtaining credit, or again, if through their
political influence they have introduced legislation particularly
favourable to wage-earners, then the economic weakness of
wage-earners as a class may very largely be removed. For
a temporary period, again, the workers in a particular industry
may be able to take advantage of the fact that their employers
have invested in large and expensive plant which they are
unwilling to leave idle, or that they possess perishable stocks of
material or have valuable business connections which they are
loth to jeopardize by letting their works stand idle.

On the other hand, circumstances are often found of a
purely economic character which abnormally restrict the freedom of the worker and in extreme cases tend virtually to
confine his choice of employment to one employer or a small
group of employers. A worker when he is bargaining individually with an employer and is not supported by a trade
union will usually be hampered by lack of information of
alternative employment or by lack of means to move about
from place to place in search of a better job : at any rate he
will probably be less well placed in these respects than will
employers, who can make enquiries by telephone, make use
of foremen and agents, and if need be send to another town
to recruit fresh " hands ". Hence the worker's choice will
generally be confined to the employment of which he has
knowledge and which is within the immediate locality. In
some cases one finds the employer owning the houses of his
employees, and so acting as their landlord as well, in which
case the employer's power over the lives of his employees
may have something of the character of the old feudal lord.
This was common in the new factory towns of a hundred
or more years ago. It survived in the countryside (until fairly

recently) in agricultural labourers' "tied cottage" and in mining villages where miners rented "company houses". Under the "truck system", which we shall mention further in Chapter III, the employer often paid his workers in vouchers on the local store owned by himself—the "tommy-shop" of which Disraeli wrote in *Sybil*. In American mining towns it is common for the company to own practically the whole town, sometimes not excluding the magistrates and police. Where this occurs, the employee may be prevented from transferring to alternative employment or refusing to accept the employer's contract for fear of losing his home, or in the other case he will be prevented from spending his wages in the cheapest market by the manner in which he is paid. Many of the schemes to lessen the "labour turnover" and to tie a worker to a particular firm, of which much is heard in America, tend to have a similar effect. Workers are frequently in a similar position of weakness whenever the existence of a large unemployed reserve gives the employer the whip-hand because he can easily fill the place of any of his workmen with fresh hands. Where, again, the industry is controlled by a monopoly, the worker who is specialized to that occupation will be virtually tied to that one employer : a situation which, in respect of the market price which the wage-earners can obtain for their labour, will be paralleled wherever any agreement exists among employers as to the terms on which they shall give employment.

§ 7. **Wages and Net Product.** From the standpoint of the owners of property the primary cost under a wage-system will consist of the wages which have to be paid to procure the necessary labour supply. For any particular employer, of course, cost will also consist of the raw material and fuel he has to buy, the "wear and tear" of machinery, and the rent he must pay and the interest on the loan-capital which he has had to borrow. His capital outlay will be distributed between the purchase of machinery (generally termed *fixed capital*) and the purchase of raw materials and labour power (generally called *circulating capital*). But, taking the system as a whole, the fundamental condition that will determine the field of investment for capital will be the abundance and cheapness of the labour supply. In each cycle of production, after part of the gross product has been set aside to repair the " wear and tear " of machinery and in the form of wages to meet the " wear and tear " of the labour supply, a surplus or net product will remain. This surplus will represent the income of employers and the return to all owners of property or of monopoly-rights and privileges of one kind or another ; and out of this surplus will be accumulated the means of raising the system to an expanded scale and so making future cycles of production larger than preceding ones. As Mrs. Marcet ingenuously remarked in her *Conversation on Political Economy* of over a century ago : " If the value produced by the labourer exceeds what he has consumed, the excess will constitute an income to his employer ; and observe, that an income can be obtained by no other means than by the employment of the poor. . . . The rich and poor are necessary to each other ; it is precisely the fable of the belly and the limbs ; without the rich the poor would starve ; without the poor the rich would be compelled to labour for their own subsistence." [1]

It will follow that the position of the masters will be the more prosperous—they will be farther removed from being " compelled to labour for their own subsistence "—the lower the costs which the system has to incur in the purchase of labour. As we shall see later, this does not necessarily mean that their prosperity will be greatest when wage-rates are as low as possible. But it does mean that the propertied class

[1] Pp. 87–8.

as a whole will gain (other things being equal) when wages, as a *proportion* of the gross product, are low; since then the proportion available as surplus or net product will be greater, and wider and more favourable opportunities for the investment of capital will exist. It will generally be true that labour will be cheaper the more dependent, and hence more compliant, is the wage-earning class, and the more plentiful is the supply (or potential supply) of labour to afford a wide and expanding field of investment. There is some historical evidence to suggest that periods in history when the supply of labour (or the potential supply) has been plentiful (relative to the capital available to exploit it) have been periods when labour has been most free from legal limitations and restrictions; and conversely with periods of labour-scarcity. But whatever the truth of any such generalization may be, it is clear that the general condition of the labour market, with its influence on the relative economic position and strength of labour and capital, will play a crucial part in determining the behaviour of the whole economic system and the economic and social policies which prevail.

CHAPTER II

WAGES AND THE STANDARD OF LIFE

§ 1. Distinctions and Definitions. Before we consider the question of wages, and of changes in wages, in connection with the working-class standard of life, there are certain preliminary distinctions which it is important to make clear.

In the first place, it is important to bear in mind the distinction between changes which may take place in the *total wages-bill* of the country as a whole and changes in the average *earnings per head* in a given period (say, a week or a month or a year). Only when the number of workers employed for wages remains the same, will a change in the one involve an equivalent change in the other. But when the number of the working population is changing, the total wages-bill and earnings per head will evidently change in different degrees, and may even move in different directions (for example, if the number of workers in employment grows by 20 per cent, and the total wages-bill grows by *less* than 20 per cent, earnings per head will actually have fallen).

In the second place, it is sometimes important to distinguish an *absolute* change in wages in either of the above senses and a change in wages *relatively* to the total output produced, or to the national income. Here one is speaking of the relative or proportionate share of wages in the total ; and it may be the case that the wages-bill of the country and also earnings per head increase, but, since the national income as a whole is increasing still faster, the relative share of wages in the total may fall. To direct one's attention to the relative share which goes as wages may be of considerable importance

16

when one is estimating the long-term trend of events : when, for instance, one is considering the effect of economic progress on the share of different classes in the total product of industry. When, however, one is looking at changes in the distribution of income, not between categories of income or classes, but between individuals, one needs to know something further than this. It is not sufficient to know how large a slice of total income goes to one class and how large a slice goes to another class or classes : one will need to know how many income-receivers there are within each class between which the slice has to be shared. If the number of wage-earners increased faster than the number of property-owners, it would be quite possible for wage-earners to be poorer (both relatively and absolutely), compared with property-owners, and hence for the inequality of incomes to increase, even though the share of the total product going in wages had increased. This would be still more likely to occur if property was becoming concentrated in fewer hands at the same time as the number of persons seeking employment in the labour market was growing. Conversely, if property-ownership was being diffused (e.g. by the splitting up of landed estates among peasant proprietors) or property was passing into the hands of the State, the distribution of income might become more equal, even though the share of the product going as wages declined.

Finally, there is the distinction to be borne in mind between changes in wages in terms of *money* and changes in wages in terms of their purchasing power over goods, or between changes in *Money Wages* and changes in *Real Wages* ; and also the distinction between changes in Wage-*Rates*, or the amount paid for a given amount or duration of work, and in the *Average Earnings* received by a worker over a given period, e.g. of a week, a month or a year. About these distinctions more will be said below.

c

§ 2. **Wages as a Proportion of Total Income.** The general features of the wage-system which were discussed in the last chapter might lead one to expect wages to be approximately the same proportion of total income in all countries where the capitalist wage-system is found. If this were the case, wages per head would be higher in those countries where the productivity of labour was higher and would tend to rise in every country as the productivity of labour increased. It has often been maintained, however, that as capitalism develops the share of the product which goes in wages is likely to decline ; since this will tend to be the effect of the progressive introduction of labour-saving machinery, and since technical change over the past century and a half has been predominantly of this type. Just as between different industries in the same country the total wages-bill as a percentage of the product of industry is apt to be high where the work is mainly manual labour and low where a large amount of mechanical horse-power is employed per man ; so one might expect the share of wages in the total product to be lower in countries where production is more highly mechanized than in countries at a more primitive technical level.

Again, one might expect labour's share in the total product to be subject to influences in the labour market such as the plentifulness or scarcity of labour, and bargaining power ; since these influences affect the price which wage-earners are able to obtain for their labour-power. The larger the reserve of labour at any time or place, the more will the labour market tend to be a " buyers' market ", and the share of labour tend to be small. Where, on the contrary, labour-power is scarce, relatively to the demand for it ; where there are relatively few barriers to prevent labourers from setting up as farmers and artisans or small employers on their own ; or where wage-earners are strongly organized in trade unions, one might expect labour to succeed in obtaining a larger share of the product than elsewhere. Other factors which may exert a powerful influence are the growth of monopolistic organization in industry, a large export of capital to colonial areas where cheap labour and natural resources are plentiful, or opportunities for the importation of cheap food supplies which increase the purchasing power of a given money-wage.

What is surprising is that the available statistics of wages as a proportion of the national income seem to show a quite remarkable stability in this proportion, both over short periods of time (such as the duration of a single trade cycle) and over longer periods. The stability is so remarkable as to have caused some persons to treat it as virtually an economic law of modern capitalist societies that the share of wages can never rise above a certain amount, even though the bargaining power of wage-earners is progressively strengthened by the growth of trade unions. The estimates of Dr. Bowley, the statistician, show that wages as a proportion of the net home-produced national income (i.e. excluding income from abroad) were approximately 39 per cent in 1880 and 39 per cent again in 1913. The highest level which they had reached over the intervening period was 41 per cent in the first half of the 1890's. In 1925 this figure had risen to 42 per cent, to fall again to 39 per cent in the middle 1930's. On the eve of the Second World War it was between 39 and 40 per cent ; and, if we exclude the pay of the armed forces from both the wage-bill and the national income, this proportion rose in the war years to no more than 41 per cent (the figure for 1943 and 1944).[1] More recently an estimate by Professor

[1] A. L. Bowley, *Wages and Income in the U.K. since 1860*, pp. 76, 92, and *Studies in the National Income*, pp. 52, 81. The wage-bill is here calculated exclusive of shop assistants. Cf. also T. Barna, *Profits* (Fabian Research Pamphlet, No. 105). Mr. Colin Clark gave 39·5 as the percentage of home-produced income less government income in 1911, 42 in 1924, 1927, 1928 and 1931–33, and 40·5 in 1935 (*National Income and Outlay*, p. 94). See also for estimates covering the whole period 1870

Sir Dennis Robertson has shown a somewhat larger change
between 1938 and 1953 in the share of wages in " net national
income at factor cost " : namely, from 40·3 per cent in 1938
to 43·6 per cent in 1953.[1] A somewhat different classification
has been made into incomes from work (a category which
includes incomes from professions and part of profits and is
considerably wider than what can be classed as wages for our
purpose) and incomes from property ; and Dr. Bowley has
estimated that the latter composed 37½ per cent of the total
national income in 1880, fell to 35–36 per cent by the end
of the century, and then rose again to 37½ per cent by 1913.[2]
As regards the U.S.A., some estimates of Dr. King show
that the relative share of wages in the net national income
rose from just under 38 per cent in 1909 to just over 40 per
cent in 1925 ; and using some figures of the American statistician Dr. Kuznets, the share of wages in the gross income
produced in private industry (i.e. excluding government
services) has been calculated by Dr. Kalecki as having been
37·2 per cent on the average of the first half of the decade
of the 1920's, 36·5 per cent between 1925 and 1929, and
35·8 per cent in the first half of the 1930's.[3] The apparent
steadiness of these figures may be, however, a coincidental
outcome of a number of influences operating in different

to 1950 : Professor E. H. Phelps Brown and P. E. Hart in *The Economic
Journal*, June, 1952, pp. 276–77.

[1] In *Wages : the Stamp Memorial Lecture for 1954*, p. 19. Pay of the
armed forces is here included in national income but excluded from
wages. Yet another estimate of wages as a percentage of gross national
product (i.e. total income without deduction of maintenance and depre-
ciation of capital) was made by Professor A. C. Pigou in *The Times* of
14 July, 1955. This showed a percentage of 36 for 1938, 40·5 for 1948
and 39·6 for 1954.

[2] *Changes in the Distribution of the National Income, 1880–1913*, p. 25.

[3] M. Kalecki, *Essays in the Theory of Economic Fluctuations*, pp. 16–17.
Whereas in the case of Britain shop assistants are excluded from the
figure of wages, in the case of U.S.A. they are included in wages.

directions: for example, shifts in the relative weight of different occupations, in each of which wages represent a different proportion of the net output; these shifts obscuring the influence of more general factors which are at work to raise or to lower labour's share in the net output of each separate line of production. Some writers, again, have laid emphasis on the degree of monopoly in the economic system (a matter to which we shall return in a later chapter) as the main determinant of the distribution of income between different income-classes in the modern world; and have suggested that the tendency for a growing degree of monopoly in the economic system at large to reduce the share of labour may have been offset by the action of other factors (partly fortuitous factors), the influence of which has been in the opposite direction.

Some estimates indicate that the share of wages in the *net* output of *manufacturing* industry shows more variation than the share of wages in the national income as a whole; as does also the share of wages in the net output of individual industries.[1] For U.S.A. two recent authorities have calculated the percentage which wages bore to the " value added by manufacture " as having been 51 per cent in 1849 and only 39 per cent in 1927.[2] There seems to be some evidence that this percentage declined throughout the 1920's and continued to do so up to 1933, after which it rose again a little in the years of President Roosevelt's New Deal; and that in Britain,

[1] Cf. J. T. Dunlop, *Wage-Determination under Trade Unions*, pp. 165–80.

[2] Douglas and Jennison, *Movement of Money and Real Earnings in the United States, 1926–28*, p. 51. If " salaries " are added to the second figure, the combined percentage for salaries and wages in 1927 comes to approximately the same as the percentages for wages alone in 1849. It must be remembered that over the three-quarters of a century between these dates there had been a large increase in the distributive trades and in commercial occupations, as well as of salaried grades in industry; so that this figure does not represent the proportion which wages and salaries bore to the total national income.

where it has been somewhat higher than in either U.S.A. or
Germany, it has shown a tendency between the wars towards
" a slow but steady decline ".[1] The share of " salaries " (as
distinct from " wages ") in the national income has shown a
marked increase from about 15·6 per cent in 1911 to 25 per
cent in 1935. Part of this increase is due to the growing
importance of clerical workers and of technical grades in
modern industry. But the major part of it apparently represents an increase among the higher categories of salary-
earners, which may be due to the progressive supersession of
the independent employer by the salaried manager of the
large concern.[2] As regards the distribution of income, not
between categories, but between persons : according to comparisons made by Pareto, this appears to have a quite surprising
similarity in all advanced capitalist countries. Just before
the Second World War, however, there was some sign that
a slightly smaller proportion of the total income was going
to the large incomes which fall within the surtax-paying class.
In the middle of the inter-war period (in 1929) those with
incomes of over £2,000 a year (comprising 0·5 per cent
of income-receivers) absorbed about 16 per cent of total
income, and those with over £1,000 about 23 per cent
of total income. By 1938 the share of this latter four-figure
class had fallen to 18 per cent.[3] To-day, of course, a
four-figure income means something very different (in

---

[1] Dr. L. Rostas on " Productivity in Britain, Germany and the United
States " in *The Economic Journal*, April, 1943, pp. 53–54.

[2] Colin Clark, *National Income and Outlay*, pp. 94, 99–101.

[3] Ibid., pp. 107–10 ; M. Abrams, *The Condition of the British People,
1911–1945*, p. 109. What is said above refers to the distribution of
income before taxation. As regards the effects of progressive taxation
of large incomes and social expenditure by the State in modifying the
pattern of income-distribution, it was estimated by Dr. Barna before
the last war that this redistribution from rich to poor in 1937 probably
amounted to some 5 or 6 per cent of the total national income (T. Barna,
Redistribution of Incomes, 1937, p. 233).

terms of real purchasing-power) from what it did in 1938, and comparisons between before and after the Second World War have to take account of the large change in the level of prices and of incomes in the intervening period. If, however, we take the share of the top 1 per cent of income-receivers in 1938 and in 1947 we find that their share (pre-tax) fell by about a third between the two dates.[1]

§ 3. Money Wages and Real Wages.   The standard of life of wage-earners will evidently remain unaffected if the money paid to them in wages is doubled but the amount available of the things which they ordinarily consume remains unchanged.   There will be shortages and queues, such as were a familiar product of swollen demand and limited supplies in wartime, and an upward pressure on prices until prices have risen as much as money-incomes (or, at least, that part of income that is *spent*) have increased.   In other words, although *money-wages* have risen, *real wages* will remain unchanged. Some persons have gone so far as to suggest that the possibility of real wages rising all round is always fairly narrowly limited by the fact that the available supply of primary food-stuffs is for the time being fairly fixed, and can only be increased after an interval of time.   It is true that after sufficient time has elapsed—perhaps a year or two years or more—the increased prices of things consumed by wage-earners may encourage capital and labour to be transferred to producing these commodities, so that their supply is ultimately increased and real wages can rise as well as money-wages.   But this will only happen if demand is not simultaneously increasing from other directions as well, and if it is only the goods consumed by wage-earners that are in short supply.   If the

---

[1] If *post*-tax income is taken, the fall is, of course, greater (namely, from a share of 12 per cent of all post-tax income to 7 per cent). See Dudley Seers in *Oxford Bulletin of Statistics*, September, 1949, p. 262.

demand from people other than wage-earners has also grown, however—either because incomes generally have increased or because well-to-do people are drawing on their bank-balances in order to spend more—prices will have a tendency to rise all round. In this case no transfer of resources into producing more of the goods consumed by wage-earners is likely to take place, and no rise in real wages will occur. In practice, of course, most of the things which wage-earners consume will be consumed by other sections of the community as well. If the prices of these things start to rise because wage-earners have more money in their pay-packets and are buying more, it may well happen that non-wage-earners (especially well-to-do people), instead of cutting down their consumption and so leaving more available to meet the higher demand from wage-earners, may simply draw on their bank-balances and increase their expenditure correspondingly in an attempt to keep their slice of the cake as large as before.[1] In other words, there is a considerable chance that people with bank-balances (and hence with a fairly inelastic demand in face of a moderate rise of prices) may so act as partly, or even wholly, to defeat the attempts of wage-earners to increase their share of the goods available by securing an increase in their money-wages.

The possibility that something of this kind may occur (unless there are price-controls in operation) is reinforced by the large amount of monopoly that exists in the economic

---

[1] If prices go up as well as wages, then profits, etc., will rise also ; and this will mean that people with bank-balances to draw upon who have increased their expenditure are likely very soon to find their income rising, which will enable them to maintain the higher level of expenditure. In other words, their initial reaction to the price-rise, if sufficiently widespread, will be " self-justifying ". If there is only a small time-interval between the initial action and its subsequent effect, bank-balances of those spending more will tend to be replenished almost as soon as they are depleted.

system of to-day. This is a matter to which we shall return in a later chapter. But if it is customary in an industry for firms to choose that combination of price and output which will yield them the maximum profit over their direct expenses of production, adding on to the latter a certain margin (whether as a percentage or as an absolute amount) in order to arrive at their selling price, then a rise in wages, and hence in direct (or prime) expenses of production, is likely to result in an equivalent stepping-up of the selling price. If demand does not rise proportionately to wages, then the output that can be sold at this higher price will tend to shrink, and may shrink so drastically as to force firms to reconsider their price-policy and to revise the profit-margin for which they allow on each unit of the commodity in a downward direction, in the interests of larger sales. But if the demand for commodities rises as well as wages and costs, for the reasons mentioned in the previous paragraph, both the higher level of prices and the previous volume of sales can be maintained ; and firms will have been successful in simply passing on the higher wage-costs in higher prices. Money-wages, prices, money profits and demand will all have risen. But, as a result, real wages and the slice of the cake which wage-earners can secure will have remained unchanged. This may possibly help to explain why the share of labour in the national income has remained so constant.

An example which has frequently been cited where money-wages rose and prices rose still faster, with the result that real wages actually fell, is the period between the closing years of the nineteenth century and the outbreak of the First World War. During this period, following increased world gold supplies and an inflow of gold into this country (coupled with a big increase of foreign investment-activity), money incomes generally increased. But the incomes of other sections of the community increased faster than wages. The result was, first of all, to raise the price of the things on which these other people spent their money—chiefly comforts and luxuries. It has been suggested that what happened in consequence of this initial price-rise was that, since luxuries were now relatively more profitable to produce, labour and capital tended to be attracted to their production away from the production of primary necessities consumed by the working class ; and this transfer of resources, by reducing the supply of goods on which wage-earners spent their money and raising their price, occasioned a fall in real wages.

In this case rising money-wages and prices seem to have been associated with falling real wages. On the basis of this example and of some others, it used to be generally supposed that prices tended always to rise faster than money-wages at times of rising prices and to fall faster than money-wages at times of falling prices ; so that the former were generally periods when real wages were falling and the latter were periods when the wage-earners' standard of life tended to rise. In recent years, however, this previously accepted view has been called in question ; and a certain amount of evidence has been collected to suggest that at times of boom and of expanding output and employment (when both prices and wages tend to be on the upward path) real wages actually rise, and that in times of slump and of contracting output and employment they are as likely to fall as to rise.[1] The evidence is not entirely conclusive, and the question remains one of some dispute. But it seems to be clear that the whole question of the connection between money-wages and real wages is a more complicated one than was formerly supposed ; and the correct answer seems to be that no single generaliza-

---

[1] Cf. J. T. Dunlop on " The Movement of Real and Money Wage Rates " in *Economic Journal*, September, 1938, and J. M. Keynes on " Relative Movements of Real Wages and Output " in *Economic Journal*. March, 1939.

tion about the connection between them holds true of all situations.[1]

§ 4. **Wage-Rates and Earnings.** When we speak of a wage-*rate*, we usually refer to the amount paid to the worker per hour or per normal working day or for performing a certain job. In other words, we are speaking about what the worker receives in return for a given output of work on his part. To measure work according to its duration may not be an accurate measure of the amount of work, in the sense of the labour-power or physical energy expended by the worker ; since the *intensity* of work (i.e. the amount of effort expended in a given time) may alter. Nor do piece-rate earnings [2] (as we shall see) always afford an adequate measure, since the amount of output for which a worker is responsible does not depend on the worker's efforts alone. Nevertheless, wage-rates per hour or per piece can be taken as *approximately* representing the price of working energy expended by the wage-earner. When we talk about the standard of life of the worker and his family, we are concerned with the total *earnings* of the family-unit over a whole week or a whole year : it is the total amount in the pay-packet that interests us in this connection, rather than the wage-rate per hour or per piece of work done. We cannot judge what is happening to the former solely from figures about the latter ; and for a number of reasons these two quantities may change quite differently.

Firstly, a worker's earnings will vary according to the number of hours for which he secures employment in the week, and according to the number of weeks of work he

---

[1] In particular the result will probably be different in a situation where *output* is changing as well as money-wages and in a situation where money-wages are changing and output is not ; and it is also likely to be affected by changes in the degree of monopoly and by simultaneous changes in the prices of imported foodstuffs and raw materials.

[2] See Chapter III.

does in the year. If a worker at one time works each day for
one or two additional hours' overtime, and at another time
does not, his earnings at the two periods will be different,
even though wage-rates per hour remain the same. At times
of bad trade, " short time " is worked in a number of industries
(for example, the cotton industry), and workers are employed
for less than the normal number of hours per day or days per
week or fortnight; while in cotton-weaving " under-employment " between the wars took the form of intermittent work
and a smaller number of looms given to each weaver to
operate. In mining it has been common for underground
workers to descend the pit for less than the full six shifts per
week, either from choice or because there is not enough work
for them to do; and in the bad years between the wars an
important reason for the poverty of mining villages was the
small number of shifts for which miners were able to obtain
employment. In 1932–33, for example, coal-mines were open
on the average for only four and a half days a week. In
the docks where men have traditionally been hired on the
" casual " system for a definite job, instead of regularly for a
whole week, only the more fortunate have managed in the
past to secure employment for the whole week or the whole
year. Between the wars the average number of days per
week worked by a docker used seldom to be much above
four, and often was less : for instance, in 1920 an average
Southampton docker worked less than three days a week.
Throughout industry at times of unemployment workers on
the average will only secure employment for less than the
normal number of weeks in the year, while some will be out
of employment for most of the months of the year or even
continually throughout the year. At such times changes in
the *earnings* of workers may be very different from the change
in wage-*rates* for a given amount of work performed.

Secondly, earnings may change in a different way from wage-rates because a movement has taken place between grades, having the result of altering the relative number in each grade. If, for example, the tendency has been for workers to be upgraded over a period, so that there are more of them in the higher-paid grades at the end of the period, as compared with the lower-paid grades, than was previously the case, the average earnings of all the workers concerned will have risen, even though the wage-rates in each grade have remained unchanged. What is true of the effect of shifts in the relative numbers in different grades is also true of the effect of shifts in the relative numbers of workers in different industries, where the wages paid differ from one industry to another.

Thirdly, earnings of workers who are paid by the piece may be affected by a change in the speed of work. The amount of work that a worker gets through in a day may change either because of greater effort exerted by himself or because of changes in the machinery or the raw material with which he works or changes in the way in which the work is organized. For example, coal-hewers may earn widely different amounts at the same tonnage wage-rate according as coal-getting at the place in the mine where they work is hard or easy. Mule-minders in spinning mills complain if they are provided with poor-quality cotton, because this retards the spinning by increasing the number of broken threads, and thereby lowers their earnings. Workers in a shoe factory or in an engineering shop may get through much more in an hour or a day, if the work is highly standardized and comes to them in " long-runs ", than if the nature of the job they have to do is continually changing and work comes to them in a large number of " short-runs ", involving frequent readjustments in the machine and in the work-process.

During the decade between 1914 and 1924, which included the industrial changes of the First World War, the influence of these factors in making earnings rise by more than wage-rates was considerable; and Dr. Bowley estimated that, while the increase in money wage-rates over the decade was between 70 and 75 per cent, the increase in average earnings, omitting the effects of unemployment, was 94 or 95 per cent.[1] Between 1924 and 1935 the movement of rates and of earnings kept in step. But during and after the Second World War the influences of which we have spoken were once more in evidence. By the end of the war, in July, 1945, wage-rates stood at 53 per cent above pre-war and average earnings of all workers at 80 per cent. This difference was mainly due to upgrading, to an increase in the number of jobs that were paid by the piece, to faster rates of output on these jobs and to the increased working of overtime and night-work. To some extent it was also due to a change in the numbers employed in different industries.[2] By 1954 wage-rates had risen above 1938 by 140 per cent, while average earnings of all workers had risen by as much as 222 per cent (of adult male workers alone by 196 per cent).[3]

But before we can calculate anything about the standard of life of the worker and his family, we have to know something more than the earnings of the individual wage-earner, and how these earnings have changed. Here the family is the unit; and one needs to know both how many earners there are to a family and how large the family is that these earnings have to support. In this respect there is room for considerable difference between different periods, between different countries and between different families. In Australia the

[1] A. L. Bowley, *Wages and Income since 1860*, pp. 11–18; also Memorandum No. 12 of the London and Cambridge Economic Service.

[2] Cf. A. L. Bowley in Memoranda Nos. 97 and 102 of the London and Cambridge Economic Service, and *Ministry of Labour Gazette*, February, 1946.

[3] London and Cambridge Economic Service Bulletins; *Ministry of Labour Gazette*, March, 1955. For wage-rates the comparison is of June, 1954 with the average of 1938; for earnings it is of the last pay-week in October, 1954 with October, 1938.

number of dependent children expressed as an average for all male wage-earners, whether married or unmarried, fathers or fatherless, in the 1920's was about 0·9, whereas in Britain it was about 1·1. In this country the average number of children per household who were under the age of fourteen had fallen between 1911 and 1931 from 1·29 to 1·1. Between different families in the same town there may be wide variations. In one family the father and perhaps two sons and a daughter may all be earning; in another a father or a widow may have to support a large number of small children and perhaps aged grandparents as well. Mr. Rowntree, in his study of the living-conditions of working-class families in York at the beginning of the century, found that nearly one-tenth of the families contained five or more dependent children, about a third contained three or more, while some two-thirds contained less than two. When this study of conditions in York was repeated, however, by Mr. Rowntree in 1936, he found that, owing to the decline in the birth-rate, the proportion of families with three or more children had declined to 9 per cent, while over three-quarters of the adult male wage-earners were either single or, if married, had less than two children dependent on them.[1] But although both the average size and the difference in size of families has changed in recent decades, it remains true that a wage which gives a fairly reasonable standard of life to an average family may mean a starvation standard for many abnormally large households which depend on one breadwinner, while a wage that is too low for an average family may leave bachelors in the same employment with a margin to spare for minor luxuries and comforts.

In measuring changes in the standard of life of wage-earners it has not always been easy in the past, on the basis of the

[1] B. Seebohm Rowntree, *Human Needs of Labour*, 1937 ed., pp. 29–30; *Poverty and Progress*, pp. 71, 483.

available statistics, to make allowance for these differences between wage-rates and earnings. Complete statistics of hourly rates of wages are not available. The Ministry of Labour has for some time collated and published monthly, in the *Ministry of Labour Gazette*, changes in the rates of wages for a large number of trades, basing these on existing collective agreements between employers and trade unions. But these figures do not cover all industries; and even in the industries to which they apply one cannot be sure that these agreements are being observed over the whole trade. The minimum rates established by Wages Councils are available in the trades where these Councils are in being. But, again, one does not know accurately how far these minima are being observed by employers generally throughout the trade, or what proportion of the workpeople are being employed above the minimum rates. There is the additional difficulty in the case of piece-workers (outside those industries where employers supply information about their total wages-bill) that even where the piece-rates are known, one cannot know how many " pieces " an average worker does in an hour or a day unless one has detailed knowledge of the industry. Formerly it was only at rather rare intervals [1] that data about average hours worked and average earnings in the main industries were collected and published. Fortunately, the Ministry of Labour has in recent years adopted the practice of collecting these data about earnings at six-monthly intervals, so that we now have much fuller information about earnings than was formerly the case. [2]

§ 5. **Index Numbers of the Cost of Living.** Difficulties further arise when from the figures of money-wages one tries to

---

[1] In 1886, 1906, 1924, 1928, 1931 and 1935.
[2] These figures of earnings are collected from some 53,000 establishments, employing about 5¼ million wage-earners.

estimate differences in real wages by making allowance for differences in the cost of living. Where the commodities consumed in the two cases which are being compared remain the same, little difficulty is involved. Information can be collected concerning a certain " sample " of actual working-class family budgets in a given year or in a given case, and an average of the various budgets in the sample can be drawn. This average budget will be made up of various commodities in different quantities—so much bread, so much meat, fuel, light, clothing, house-room and so forth. Then the cost of purchasing this average budget in the two cases can be calculated, and the difference of cost expressed as an *index number*, with the figure in one case (called " the base ") for convenience expressed as = 100. For instance, one might have an index number of the cost of living represented in the two cases thus :

(1)   100
(2)   120

The two cases might be either two countries or two years between which a comparison was being made. Then the difference of money-wages in the two cases could be divided by the difference in the index number of the cost of living, and the relation of real wages in the two cases could thus be obtained. For instance, if wages between two periods rose from 40s. to 48s. and the cost of living index number from 100 to 120, real wages would have remained unchanged.

But, in actual practice the various items which go to make up a family budget seldom are the same at two different periods and in two different countries. Different commodities have different importance in the two cases. One commodity will appear in one and an alternative or substitute in another. Over a certain period families may give up eating butter and take to margarine ; they may eat less ham and

D

more beef ; they may spend less on beer and more on clothes. In Britain working-class families drink tea : on the Continent they drink coffee. In some countries white wheaten bread is eaten : in others rye bread is the staple diet or potatoes and potato flour. In Eastern countries workers subsist mainly on rice. In the worker's diet in overseas countries eggs are six times as important as in Central Europe, and in Scandinavian countries milk and milk products bulk much larger than in England. When it comes to other things than food, such as clothes, furniture, house-room, the qualities differ considerably in the various cases, and it is virtually impossible to express these differences quantitatively. Is a pound of tea to be regarded as equivalent to a pound of coffee, a pound of wheaten bread to a pound of rye bread, a pound of butter to a pound of margarine, a pair of boots bought by an English worker to a pair of sandals bought by a Chinese coolie—or to two pairs of sandals, or three pairs or what ? Just after the First World War one found Professor Bowley, on the one hand, claiming that the official cost of living index number *over*-estimated the rise in prices because in practice people had altered their habits and transferred to cheaper substitutes (e.g. from butter to margarine) ; while on the other hand complaints came from the trade unions that the official figure *under*-estimated the rise, since it took no account of deterioration in the quality of the things which were bought and gave too little " weight " or importance to things like clothing which had risen in price more than the average. It has sometimes been suggested that the difficulty could be overcome by taking a standard of calories, or food values, and equating different articles on the basis of the number of calories that they severally contain. But it seems doubtful whether this would suffice even when one was dealing only with food : in the light of the recent emphasis by scientists on a balance of vitamins and minerals in the diet an estimate of calories alone would clearly be incomplete. For anything else than food, where psychological as well as purely physiological considerations come in, a physical standard of this kind could not assist us.

The fundamental difficulty is that the " standard of life " which one is seeking to compare is hardly a quantity and cannot be precisely measured. We may define a " standard of life " objectively as consisting in the satisfaction of certain physiological and psychological needs,[1] or subjectively as consisting in a certain degree of happiness or satisfaction of desires ; but in either case, although the standard is something which can be spoken of as being greater or less and so can be compared, it is not possible to express this as greater or less by a given amount. Hence, when we try to measure and to express the standard of life in figures, we are fitting an unmeasurable thing to a certain scale of our own, just as when an examiner tries to compare the intelligence of his examinees by allotting marks to them. In either case the precise way we fit what we are trying to compare into our scale of comparison must be largely arbitrary. All we can do is to ensure that we do not place the various items in the wrong order in the scale and that we reduce the possibility of error to a minimum.

The simplest way of handling the situation is to take the budget of any given time or any given country, and to compare the cost of buying that *same budget* at other times or in other countries. This is what is done by the Ministry of Labour Cost of Living Index Number in this country, which rests on a sample budget in a given " base year " ; and it was also done in an enquiry into the cost of living in various

[1] Perhaps " needs " are a quantity although " desires " are not. But even if physiological needs are capable of being expressed quantitatively in calories or something of the sort, psychological needs at present are not.

countries undertaken by the British Board of Trade in 1905–9, which adopted an average English budget and enquired as to the cost of that budget in various countries. This method is quite satisfactory where the *actual* budget does not differ very much in the cases under comparison. But where the budget consumed in practice varies at all considerably, quite odd and contradictory results may be found, according as one adopts one or other of the different budgets as basis. For instance, the International Labour Office of the League of Nations in 1924 investigated how much could be purchased by a carpenter's wages in various capital cities. When it took the cost in Stockholm of the food items which a *British* family consumed, it found that a Swedish carpenter's wages purchased 8 per cent *less* than a British carpenter's wage could buy in London. But when it took the food items which the *Swedish* family ordinarily consumed, it found that a Swedish carpenter's wages could purchase 9 per cent *more* of them in Stockholm than a British carpenter's wage could purchase of the same things in London. The one method showed real wages in Stockholm to be 8 per cent lower than in London, the other method 9 per cent higher. Similarly a Berlin carpenter's real wage was by one method shown to be 46·3 per cent of the London carpenter's, and 53·6 per cent by the other method.

This difficulty can be surmounted again by an arbitrary device, which amounts simply to an averaging of the results obtained by the different methods. In comparing real wages in the same place at different times what is called the " chain " method is often suggested. The cost of living in 1914, for instance, may be compared with that in 1913 on the basis of the actual 1913 budget, and then 1915 compared with 1914 on the basis of the 1914 budget, and so on. The chief difficulty is here a practical one : the method is complicated and requires a continual revision of the budget on which the calculation is based. In the international comparison of real wages which was started by the British Ministry of Labour in 1923 and then continued by the International Labour Office in 1924 a series of " baskets ", or budgets, of various foodstuffs was adopted, each " basket " being composed of different items of food in the proportion in which they enter into working-class consumption in a particular group of countries. The cost in each of various cities—London, Berlin, Stockholm, Paris, Philadelphia, etc.—of buying each of these national " baskets " was calculated—the English basket, the Scandinavian, the Central European. The cost of these several " baskets " was then compared with the wages in the various cities and expressed as a percentage ; and the results for each city were averaged and taken as the index number of real wages for that city. As an instance of the method we have a comparison between three cities as follows :

RATIO OF THE NUMBER OF TIMES A CARPENTER'S WAGES IN
DIFFERENT CITIES WILL PURCHASE

	The British basket.	The Scandinavian basket.	The Central European basket.	Average.
In London . .	100	100	100	100
„ Stockholm .	92·0	109·0	91·4	97·4
„ Berlin . .	46·3	53·6	49·3	49·7

The official (Ministry of Labour) index number of the cost of living in this country continued until after the Second World War to be based on a pattern of expenditure derived from enquiries into working-class family budgets which had been made prior to the First World War. Thus the " weight ", or relative importance, attached to various items of expenditure was very different from the actual importance which they had in household expenditure in the forties. For example, in this old index the food-items included covered only two-thirds of the actual food-consumption of an average working-class family on the eve of the Second World War : fruit and vegetables other than potatoes were omitted, candles were assumed to be the main lighting and not electricity, and unbleached cotton and calico were prominent as articles of clothing but not rayon. It is hardly surprising that during the war years the official index should have registered no more than a 31 per cent rise (from September 1939 to June, 1947), whereas the " true " rise (as calculated by Professor R. G. D. Allen on the basis of actual pre-war expenditure) was of the order of 70 per cent.

In June, 1947 a new " interim " index number was introduced, based on a budget enquiry conducted just before the war. The " weights " shown by this pre-war enquiry were adjusted according to the relative price-changes of the items in question since the enquiry was conducted ; and for this new index the price-level in June, 1947 was taken as " base " and expressed as = 100. In January, 1952 a further change was made ; the weights being revised in the light of the estimated consumption-pattern of 1950 adjusted to the prices ruling in January, 1952. The change was introduced, however, in such a way as to make the revised index continuous with the preceding one, and using the same base as before (namely, June, 1947). At the time of writing this remains the basis for calculating the (weighted) average percentage change in the level of prices each month.

The following table enables one to compare at a glance the " weights " (expressed in percentages) of the main categories of expenditure as used in the old index prior to 1947, in the " interim index " between 1947 and 1952 and since February, 1952.

	Old Index.	" Interim Index " 1947.	1952.
Food	60	34·8	39·9
Rent and Rates	16	8·8	7·2
Clothing	12	9·7	9·8
Fuel and Light	8	6·5	6·6
Household Durables . .	⎫	7·1	6·2
Miscellaneous Goods . . .	⎪	3·5	4·4
Services	⎬ 4	7·9	9·1
Drink	⎪	⎱ 21·7	⎱ 7·8
Tobacco	⎭	⎰	⎰ 9·0
	100	100	100

§ 6. Movements in Real Wages. Prior to the present century the data for a study of wage-movements were very incomplete. Index numbers of changes in retail prices did not exist in the nineteenth century, and use has to be made of estimates based on such price-records as exist. For changes in money-wages over the nineteenth century Dr. Bowley has compiled the following index number.

1800–10	.	.	.	. 55–65
1820–30	.	.	.	. 65
1840–50	.	.	.	. 60
1860–70	.	.	.	. 75
1870–80	.	.	.	. 95
1880–90	.	.	.	. 90
1890–99	.	.	.	. 100

To convert this into an index of real wages, we have to take account of the fact that prices in general approximately halved between 1800 and 1900; falling up to 1848, then rising by about 14 per cent up to 1860, and falling again between 1870 and the middle 1890's by about 25 per cent. It, therefore, looks as though real wages may have increased between three and four times over the century. This rise in real wages began to reach a standstill about the turn of the century, and after 1900 to give place to a downward tendency as prices rose again between 1896 and 1914. In these seventeen or eighteen years before the First World War money-wages, while they rose, lagged behind prices.

During the inflation of the war years, with its rapid rise of prices, money wage-rates again lagged behind prices in their rise; although, due to the factors that we have mentioned above (§ 4), money earnings rose to a considerably greater extent than did wage-rates. In the two years immediately following the war the workers were able to take advantage of a comparatively strong bargaining position and of the removal of war-time restrictions on trade union activities to make up some of the leeway they had lost. As a result, by the end of 1920 and the beginning of 1921, when prices were beginning to fall again, real wage-rates probably stood at rather more than 5 per cent above the 1914 level. By 1924 real wage-rates stood at about the same level as before the war; but average real earnings somewhat above pre-war by about 12 per cent—an increase which was approximately offset by the high level of unemployment prevailing in the 1920's compared with the immediate pre-war years.

In the years following 1929 prices underwent a further decline, especially the prices of imported foodstuffs; and compared with a fall in the cost of living between 1929 and 1933 of some 15 per cent, money-wages fell by only 5 or 6 per cent; so that the real wages of those who retained their jobs in these years of mounting unemployment showed a sharp rise. By the end of the thirties the cost of living had risen again to about 90 per cent of the level prevailing in 1924. But

wage-rates had also risen ; so that on the eve of the Second
World War real wage-rates were some 15 or 16 per cent and
average real earnings some 21 per cent above 1924.[1]

This meant that, allowing for the effects of greater unemployment on working-class earnings as a whole, the average level
of real earnings of the working class had risen since the early
part of the century by rather more than a quarter.   Over the
same period there had taken place a reduction of about
10 per cent in the hours worked in a normal working week
in most industries, so that workers as a whole were enjoying
more leisure.   On the other hand, the intensity of work—the
expenditure of labour-power demanded of a worker within
each working hour—had also increased in a large number of
industries, as a result of new mechanical processes, involving
greater strain, and speed-up devices.   In the five years between
1924 and 1929 alone the output per worker rose by some
10 per cent ; and it has been estimated by Mr. Colin Clark
that the output per worker by the middle thirties was between
15 and 20 per cent greater than twenty-five years before.[2]
Another estimate has placed the increased output per worker
at 12 per cent between 1924 and 1930 and another 10 to
11 per cent between 1930 and 1934.[3]   How much of this
increase is attributable to new mechanical devices which do
not involve increased strain or exertion for manual labour,
and how far it indicates that the production process has
become more exacting of human labour-power is not easy
to calculate.   But the fact that the intensity of work has

[1] London and Cambridge Economic Service Bulletins ; A. C. Pigou,
Wage Statistics and Wage Policy (the Stamp Memorial Lecture for 1949),
pp. 7–9.   [2] *National Income and Outlay*, p. 269.
[3] Witt Bowden, " The Productivity of Labour in G.B.", in *The Journal
of Political Economy*, June, 1937.   The comparison between 1924 and
1930 relates to industries included in the census of production for G.B.
and N.I., and that between 1930 and 1934 to industries included in the
Production Index of the Board of Trade.

been increased in some degree, whether large or small, must clearly be taken into account.

A marked contrast between the First and the Second World War was the much smaller price-rise that occurred during the latter. This was due to the greater extent and efficacy of price-controls and rationing, combined with a government policy of subsidizing an " iron ration " of basic necessities in order to keep their cost from rising. The official cost-of-living index registered a rise of no more than 33 per cent above pre-war (summer 1945). This index, however, tended (as we have seen) to underweight the more expensive foodstuffs and sundry items which had risen in price much more, and took no account of war-time shifts in expenditure, due to rationing, towards more expensive unrationed commodities. The so-called " Treasury index " of retail prices in general showed a rise of 54 per cent ; and there is reason to suppose that the " true " rise in the cost of living of wage-earners was much closer to the latter figure than to the former.[1] Meanwhile the rise in wage-rates up to the end of the war in Europe was about 50 per cent, and the rise in earnings (allowing for the various factors we mentioned in § 4) was about 80 per cent. It seems probable, therefore, that the real wage-rates paid for a given quantity of work and type of job remained approximately constant over the war years, but that, when we take account of such things as overtime, upgrading and increased output on jobs paid by the piece, the real value of the weekly pay-packet may have increased on the average by some 20 per cent. Since the end of the

[1] A calculation by Mr. J. L. Nicholson in the *Bulletin* of the Oxford Institute of Statistics (13 October, 1945) of a " wage-earners' index " indicated a 50 per cent rise in 1944 over 1938. This took account of the effects both of subsidies and of indirect taxes on market prices. But Mr. Nicholson pointed out that his index made no allowance " for the effects of rationing and shortages in reducing the consumer's freedom of choice ".

War the movement of wage-rates and the cost of living have continued to keep fairly closely in step, while average earnings have again kept ahead ; a recent estimate of Professor A. C. Pigou showing real wage rates in 1954 as 3 per cent only above 1938 and " average real earnings of wage-earners at work " as 21 per cent above 1938.[1]

So far we have been talking mainly of averages. But some may doubt whether average figures of real earnings have much significance over a period in which large changes have taken place in the relation between earnings in different grades and in different industries and localities. Outstanding among such changes in the inter-war period were the narrowing of the gap between skilled and unskilled wages as compared with the pre-1914 period and the considerable disparity between wage-movements in the more prosperous and expanding industries (largely producing for the home market) and in the depressed trades (largely export trades) where employment was sharply contracting. During and after the Second World War the difference between skilled and unskilled wages was narrowed still further, as can be seen from the following table showing the time-rates for unskilled workers as a percentage of those for skilled workers in 1914, in 1920, in 1939 and in 1950.[2]

	Building.	Shipbuilding.	Engineering.	Railways.
1914	66·5	55·2	58·6	54·3
1920	81·0	77·2	78·9	81·2
1939	76·3	73·4	75·6	61·5
1950	84·1	81·7	84·7	77·4

[1] Article in *The Times*, 13 July, 1955. Taking account of the much smaller unemployment of the post-war period, Professor Pigou goes on to estimate " average real earnings of wage-earners at work and unemployed " as having increased by 32 per cent over 1938.

[2] From article by K. G. J. C. Knowles and D. J. Robertson in *Oxford Bulletin of Statistics*, April, 1951, p. 111.

As regards wage-movements in various industries, several of
the previously depressed industries, especially coal-mining and
agriculture, and to a less extent cotton, have benefited from
the increased demand for labour in those industries during
or after the war and have markedly improved their relative
position compared both with the average and with occupations such as railways and some other branches of transport
where wage-rates and earnings have lagged behind the average
movement since before the Second World War.

§ 7. **Poverty.** Before the First World War Mr. Seebohm
Rowntree conducted an investigation into the wages necessary
for a worker with a wife and three children to maintain a
minimum standard of life. The standard that Mr. Rowntree
adopted in his original investigation in 1899 into the state
of poverty in the city of York [1] was a minimum standard of
bare physical existence, below which the family could be said
to be in starvation or semi-starvation. It represented largely
a vegetarian diet; it provided for the clothing of children,
for example, only half what Poor Law Institutions spend on
clothing children under their charge; and allowed nothing
for railway- or tram-fares or such things as newspapers and
tobacco. Later Mr. Rowntree worked out a second standard,
which included certain minor comforts, and was defined as a
standard of decent existence and of minimum human needs,
below which a worker's family, though not actually starving,
could be said to be in poverty—a standard " below which no
class of worker should be forced to live ".[2] At the prices
ruling in 1914 the weekly wage which he estimated as necessary
to maintain the first standard was 26s., and that necessary
to maintain the second standard was 35s. 3d. At the prices
ruling at the end of the Second World War the equivalent

---

[1] Cf. *Poverty: a Study of Town Life.*
[2] Cf. *The Human Needs of Labour.*

figures would lie somewhere between 45s. and 50s. in the first
case and between 65s. and 75s. in the second case. Similar
investigations were subsequently made in U.S.A. and Australia, which adopted standards from 15 to 25 per cent higher
than those of Mr. Rowntree. In the course of the 1930's
Mr. Rowntree revised slightly the food requirements for his
" human needs " standard in the light of scientific studies in
human nutrition in recent years, and calculated that 53s. 9d.
was required to purchase this standard at the prices ruling
in 1936. It is to be noted that this standard is a strictly
modest one, and while it allows a sum of 9s. per week for
" sundries " such as insurance contributions, fares, newspapers, tobacco and recreation, it allows only for the consumption of condensed, and not of fresh, milk, and represents
a standard of consumption for the unskilled labourer based
on the assumption that he is performing " moderate ", but
not " hard ", work, and containing about half of the nutriment
of a sedentary West End clubman. In 1906-7, according to
the Board of Trade wage census of that year, the *average*
earnings of male workers were below Mr. Rowntree's " human
needs " standard, though considerably above his lower starvation standard. Of the lower-paid workers a large proportion
must have fallen below the lower minimum : in his investigation in York Mr. Rowntree found that the earnings of 15 per
cent of working-class families were insufficient to maintain
this purely physical standard. According to an investigation
conducted by the Ministry of Labour into weekly earnings
in 1935, the earnings of miners in a number of colliery districts a little more than covered this lower standard, but fell
short by nearly 10s. of Mr. Rowntree's revised human
needs standard ; average earnings in the textile and clothing
industries (which include the earnings of a large number of
women workers) barely sufficed to obtain the lower standard ;
in the leather industry they were some 8s. above it, but

some 5s. below the higher standard; in shipbuilding and
engineering they were just above the human needs standard,
and in printing and paper and building several shillings
above.

In the period between the wars it was the large volume
of unemployment and the plight of the depressed trades like
coal, textiles, shipbuilding and marine engineering that were
primarily responsible for poverty, and operated to worsen the
working-class standard of life in the distressed areas. At the
same time there were two influences at work whose influence
was in the opposite direction: to lessen the percentage of
families who fell below the poverty line. First of these was
the institution of minimum rates for a number of the lowest-
paid trades under the Trade Board system, which had extended
considerably in the immediate post-war years. The second
was the effect of the declining birth-rate in reducing the
number of children to be supported from the earnings of a
family. Between 1911 and 1931 the number of children under
fifteen as a percentage of the total population of England
and Wales fell from 30·6 to 25·6; and the proportion of all
families having four or more dependent children fell from
one-third to one-fifth. Since it is the large families among
the working class that are most likely to fall below the poverty
line, this reduction in the number of large families had an
appreciable effect on the percentage of families in poverty.
Partly offsetting this was the fact that, with the shift in the
age-composition of the population as a result of a much
slackened rate of population-increase, the older generation
past working age, which has to be supported by their children,
had tended to become larger relatively to the new generation
than was formerly the case.

Dr. Bowley in an investigation, undertaken in 1913 and
repeated in 1924,[1] into a sample of families in a sample of

¹ *Has Poverty Diminished?*, by Bowley and Hogg.

industrial towns adopted a starvation standard closely similar to that of Mr. Rowntree. The investigation was concerned only with what the latter had termed " primary poverty " : cases where earnings were absolutely insufficient to maintain this standard even if the whole of them had been spent on items included in the standard and on nothing else. In 1913 he found that in 11–12 per cent of the families earnings were below what was necessary to maintain this standard. In 1924 the investigators reported a definite improvement in the position : an improvement that was attributed to a decline in the number of dependent children per family and to the relatively greater improvement in the position of the lowest-paid workers as compared with the average of all wage-earners. *If* all the wage-earners in the families investigated had been in full employment, the proportion of families definitely below the standard would have been between 3·6 and 4·7 per cent. In the actual week of the investigation, owing to unemployment and short-time, between 6·5 and 8 per cent were below the standard. It has to be remembered, however, that as regards unemployment the year 1924 was a comparatively good year among the between-the-wars years (the average unemployment percentage for the whole year only being lower in one year between 1920 and 1939, and only as low in 1929 and again in 1939). *The New Survey of Life and Labour in London*, using a standard for food that was below what a committee of the British Medical Association had stated to be a minimum for health and working efficiency, recorded a poverty-figure of between 9 and 10 per cent of working-class families in the year 1928 (another comparatively good year so far as employment was concerned). About the same time surveys conducted in the more depressed areas of the north recorded substantially higher percentages than this : in 1929 Surveys in Merseyside and Liverpool, using the same low standard as the London Survey, found that respectively

17 and 16 per cent of the working-class families were living in poverty. Southampton in the bad year of 1931 recorded a figure of 20 per cent. Investigators in Bristol found that even in the good year of 1937 between 10 and 11 per cent of working-class families were below the B.M.A. standard. Mr. Rowntree, in his new Survey of York in 1935–6, found that " primary poverty " was only half what it had been at the time of his first investigation at the beginning of the century, and that unemployment had taken the place of low wages as the principal cause of poverty. Nevertheless, in that relatively prosperous year 31 per cent of the families were below the level of his " human needs standard ".

Yet a further Rowntree study, conducted over the same ground, was undertaken after the Second World War, in 1950 (and published in 1951 as *Poverty and the Welfare State* by B. Seebohm Rowntree and G. R. Lavers). This showed a remarkable improvement, due almost entirely to the virtual abolition of unemployment and to post-war " welfare legislation " (in which term there was included the food subsidies, family allowances, provision of milk to schoolchildren and infants and school meals). Whereas in the previous investigation some 31 per cent of working-class families had been in " primary poverty " judged by the " human needs standard ", in 1950 the equivalent percentage was under 5 per cent (and even less expressed as a percentage of *persons* instead of as a percentage of families). Old age had taken the place of unemployment and low wages as the leading cause of poverty. It should be noted, however, that a substantial proportion of the families investigated were no more than a few shillings above the poverty-line adopted in this study (as many as 8 per cent were above it by less than 6s. per week) ; so that it would have needed only a slight upward adjustment of the " minimum standard ", or alternatively a small adverse change of circumstances, to have raised the poverty-percentage appreciably.[1] Even so there would still have been a substantial improvement on the position of the 1930's.

One feature of poverty that has been specially stressed in the past by social investigators is its special incidence upon the young (and consequently on the health of the next generation). This was because the larger families were apt to be those which fell into poverty, and accordingly a larger proportion of *children* at any one time than of adults or of families were below the poverty-line. In his 1935–36 study in York, Mr. Rowntree estimated that nearly a half of all working-class children were still liable to be under-nourished for a period of five years or more of their childhood, and nearly a third of them for a period of as long as ten years or more. The falling birth-rate, with its smaller families, has tended to relieve this problem ; and the system of children's allowances, introduced in 1946 as part of the new national insurance scheme after the war, was designed specifically to deal with this aspect of a grave social evil.

[1] If the poverty-line for an " average family " had been raised from £5 to £5 6s. (exclusive of rent), the poverty-percentage would have been 12 per cent instead of 4·6 (see a review by the present writer in *The Economic Journal*, March, 1952, pp. 173–75).

E

CHAPTER III

THE PAYMENT OF WAGES

§ 1. Wages and Cost of Production. The supposition that low wages mean cheap production and that high wages cause high prices long ago became a stock example of an economic fallacy to which the unthinking mind is prone. Yet it is a fallacy which dies hard ; and even economic writers, who are sometimes too fond of using an index of real wages as an index of labour-cost of production, cannot be entirely acquitted of this mistake. But as we have seen in the previous chapter, there are a number of reasons why a movement in wage-rates or earnings and a movement in labour-cost may be far from coincidental.

When we speak of the labour-cost of producing a given output, we may mean either of two things. First, we may mean the actual amount of work or human energy put into production. Secondly, we may mean the money that the employer has had to lay out in wages to get the output produced—his wage-outlay. It would, perhaps, be clearer if the term " labour-cost " were confined to the former, and some such term as wage-cost used instead for the latter. At any rate, it should be clear that labour-cost in our first sense *may* be quite independent of the level of wages, and need not be affected by any change of wages. It is the inverse of the physical productivity of labour, and will depend on the skill of the worker in handling his job and upon the nature and efficiency of the mechanical equipment with which he works. On the other hand, the wage-cost of producing anything will depend *both* upon the productivity of labour *and* upon the level of wages, and will be changed by a change in either of these things. Changes in them will have opposite effects ; a rise in wages raising and a rise in productivity lowering the wage-cost of producing a given output. A rise in wages, therefore, will not involve any increase of cost *if* it is accompanied by an equivalent increase in the efficiency of labour. There is a further case to be borne in mind where a rise in wages may not involve any increase in the cost of production : namely, where there is a rise, not of money wages, but of real wages due to a fall in the price of things consumed by wage-earners. For example, much of the increase in real wages in the course of the nineteenth century was of this character, being due to the differential cheapening of imported food supplies, and for this reason did not involve any equivalent increase in wage-cost to industry.

But it was also the case that the productivity of labour increased considerably in the nineteenth century ; and accordingly, although money wage-rates by 1900 were nearly twice as high as they had been in 1800, there is no reason to suppose that the wage-cost of producing a bushel of corn, a ton of iron, or a pair of boots had also doubled, or that it had even risen at all. Nor does it follow, because the wages received by an Asiatic worker are only a quarter or a fifth of those received by his equivalent in this country, that Asiatic products must drive the wares of Manchester or Birmingham, Bradford or Dundee, from the markets of the world : the productivity of labour in the two cases may vary in like degree. It is clear, therefore, that high and low wages *may* be associated with high and low efficiency. The important question remains as to whether there is any reason to expect that they will be associated in this way. It was to this connection between the wage-level and efficiency that Lord Brassey drew attention when in the middle of last century he enunciated the principle that came to be known as the " economy of high wages ". As one example among many of his contention that " it is quite possible that work may be more cheaply executed by the same workmen, notwithstanding that their wages have increased ", he cited a comparison between the wage-cost of railway-construction in Ireland and in England. While the day-wages paid to navvies employed by his father's agent on building the South Staffordshire Railway were double those paid by the same agent two years later in constructing a line in Ireland, " yet, with this immense difference in the rate of wages, sub-contracts on the Irish Railway were let at the same prices which had been previously paid in Staffordshire ".[1]

The reason for the connection between high wages and high efficiency is not far to seek. If a worker and his family live at a high standard, their health and their physical and mental vigour will be much higher than in the case of a family that is poverty-stricken and undernourished. It has recently been shown that there is a marked difference between the liability to disease and even the height and other bodily measurements of children who come from rich and from poor homes ; and what is true of differences of health and physique is also true of differences of working efficiency. But there are two cautions to be borne in mind in applying this important principle. It by no means follows from this principle that it will be in the interest of employers to pay their men high wages since a high wage means a high efficiency. Sometimes they may feel it a good investment to do so ; just as an employer who manufactures goods which serve a working-class demand may feel it good business to preach high wages all round, and to set the example of what he preaches by paying high wages himself. But the reactions of a high standard of life on efficiency are not instantaneous : many of them show themselves only after a considerable lapse of time ; and some of the most important show their effect

[1] *Work and Wages*, 69. Cf. also his *Foreign Work and English Wages.*

only on the next generation through the reaction of better nourishment and healthier conditions on the children. An individual employer is not going to find it profitable to pay higher wages in order that some years hence another employer, or another generation of employers, shall reap the fruit of increased human efficiency. In other words, since under a free wage-system the employer merely hires labour-power for a temporary period, and no longer owns the person of the labourer or even has a permanent lien on his services, he may have less regard for the personal welfare of his workers than would be the case under a slave-system. This has been adduced as the crucial reason for State support of trade unions and for the imposition of a minimum living-wage by the State. Nor does it necessarily follow that the increase of efficiency is *proportional* to the increased wage. For workers near the poverty-level this may well be the case ; and for workers who are undernourished, and haunted by degrading living-conditions and the fear of unemployment, a given increase in their standard of living may result in a disproportionately large improvement in their working efficiency. But one must avoid exaggerating this principle when applying it to workers on a standard of life that is appreciably above the poverty-line. As the recent researches of scientists have shown, with their emphasis on animal protein and various minerals in the diet, the level of income at which increased expenditure on food, particularly on the more expensive foodstuffs, brings increased health and efficiency is probably much higher than was formerly thought. But as the standard of life rises, the increase of efficiency which follows a further raising of that standard gets proportionately smaller, and our principle applies with diminishing force. The principle, therefore, does not suffice to prove that the class of employers can continue to raise wages indefinitely and find that they are repaid by the resulting increase of

efficiency. Yet this seems to have been the view of certain
writers who were so impressed with American prosperity in
the years between 1922 and 1929 as to attribute it mainly or
entirely to the high level of American wages, and to preach
high wages as the millennial cure of all economic ills.

§ 2. **Wage-payment and Incentive.** There is another aspect of
the connection between wages and work, other than the
physiological; namely, that of *inducement.* What we have
so far been considering has concerned the workers' ability
to work. But a change in wages may affect the willingness to
work more or less intensively or for longer or shorter periods
of time. Here it does not seem to be the case, however, that
the correlation between the wage-level and the amount of
work performed is a positive one; and there is some evidence
that it may be negative.[1] In unusually laborious and unpleasant
occupations such as coal-mining this is likely to be specially
marked, as it will be also in the case of women and old
workers, who may be disinclined to seek employment unless
the pressure of circumstances forces them to do so. The
reason for this is that as the wage-level increases the worker
may prefer to take advantage of the benefit in the form of
greater leisure rather than of an increase in money earnings [2];
while on the other hand workers on a very low standard of
life may be forced by the pressure of poverty into working
laboriously for long hours as the only means of earning enough
to purchase the bare necessities of life (a reason, as we shall
see, why the exploitation of workers at a low standard of life

[1] Professor Paul Douglas has adduced statistical evidence from American experience to suggest that the short-period elasticity of supply of
labour is negative and about -0.3 (*Theory of Wages*, 274–89, 302–13).

[2] This tendency to sacrifice increased earnings to increased leisure may
not in fact be as strong as is often supposed, since the demand for income
and the demand for leisure is so largely a " joint demand "—to enjoy
more leisure one usually needs to have a larger income.

may be cumulative). This view of the matter seems to have been exclusively held by earlier centuries, to the neglect of other considerations ; one seventeenth-century writer dismissing high wages with the remark, " they work so much the fewer days by how much more they exact in wages ", and an eighteenth-century writer (Arthur Young) more forcibly adding : " Everyone but an idiot knows that the lower classes must be kept poor or they will never be industrious." But what is probably more important than the rate of wages, with respect to incentive, is the *method* of wage-payment. If wages are paid on a piece-rate instead of a time-rate basis—in proportion to the " pieces " done, or " by results "—a special inducement will be given to the worker to increase the speed at which he works in order that he may earn more in a given time. The discussion that has taken place over the various systems of wage-payment which have been devised and are in use has been concerned primarily with this question of incentive. But while there is clearly a strong advantage to an employer in basing his wage-system on some form of " payment by results ", this advantage is not necessarily as great as might at first sight appear ; nor does it necessarily follow that it will profit him to pay high rather than low piece-rates as an inducement to larger output. For, while thereby he may get extra output to sell, he also has to pay extra in wages to get it, and, when the payment is on a " straight " piece-rate basis, to pay proportionately more in wages to get it. It is this which has led (as we shall see) to the invention of more complex systems of wage-payment, which have the effect of increasing the remuneration for greater output, but increasing it at a *smaller* (and generally a diminishing) rate than the speed of work is increased.

§ 3. **Piece-rates and " Speed-up ".** It is sometimes said that while the employer is interested in securing a low wage-cost, the worker is interested in securing a high level of earnings, and that, since by increased efficiency both things can be simultaneously attained, employer and worker should have a like interest in the speeding-up of work and in all methods which promote this result. In the past a similar, but more general, argument has been advanced to the effect that anything which hinders an increase of output is damaging to worker and employer alike ; and trade unionists in the nineteenth century were severely castigated by economists for adhering, it was alleged, to a vicious " Work Fund " fallacy, which held that there was a limited amount of work to go round and that workers could benefit themselves by restricting the amount of work they did. But the argument as it stands is incorrect. It is not aggregate earnings which are the measure of the benefit obtained by the worker, but his earnings in relation to the work he does—to his output of physical energy or his bodily wear and tear.[1] Just as an employer is interested in his receipts compared with his outgoings, so the worker is presumably interested in what he gets compared with what he gives. A man who works longer hours or is put on piece-rates, and increases the intensity of his work as a result, may earn more money in the course of the week ; but he is also suffering more fatigue, and probably requires to spend more on food and recreation and perhaps on doctor's bills. Workers, for instance, who are working at the intensity of Western factory methods usually require a meat diet, while more leisurely toiling Eastern workers can subsist on a cereal diet and probably could not stand more intensive methods of work on the diet which is their lot. Moreover, there is evidence that piece-workers (as Adam Smith observed) are often induced by the attraction of immediate earnings to

[1] I.e. it will be to his interest to make the aggregate difference between what he earns and the effort he expends (so far as this is measurable) as large as possible.

accelerate their work to a point which is detrimental to their health in the long run and may seriously shorten the length of their working life. The many disputes which have occurred over the adoption of methods which have " speed-up " as their objective are therefore by no means founded on pure illusion.

In general, therefore, one can say that the employer will have a greater interest in the extension of working hours and in increased intensity of work than will his employees. But there is a special reason that will make it advantageous to the employer to get the maximum output that he can out of each man. This consists in the additional economies which he can obtain from more intensive use of his machinery : from the fact that to extract a larger output from his factory in a given period is to make each machine do more work and so to economize on the " overhead cost " of this machine. To a certain extent the same would apply if the increased output was obtained by employing a larger staff of workpeople in the workshop. But the point where it ceases to be profitable to extend the use of existing plant by this method—by crowding more men on to each machine—comes much sooner than it does when the same number of men are employed and each man works more quickly or works overtime at the end of the day when otherwise the plant would be idle. Where it is practicable to introduce a multiple-shift system— two or three working-shifts a day instead of one—the same economy could be obtained together with the employment of additional workers. But where this is not practicable, or where its potentialities have already been exploited, the employer will find it profitable to increase the speed of his existing workers rather than to increase the number of hands he employs. The economy of this consists in the fact that, while the increased work that is done may require more circulating capital (for materials and wages) to finance it, the

cost of the fixed capital (save for a small but far from equivalent
addition to the wear-and-tear of machinery) will remain the
same.   Hence while the employer's profit may increase in
no greater proportion than his circulating capital has had
to be increased,[1] it will tend to increase in proportion to the
total capital in use (circulating *plus* fixed) and his profits as
a percentage of his total capital will consequently tend to
rise.   It is this fact which, in part, explains why it may even
be profitable for employers (within limits) to raise piece-rates
in order thereby to stimulate higher speeds of work (as is
explicitly provided for under such a system as the " differential
piece-rate ") : employers may gain more in economy of plant
and machinery than they lose in having to pay out more in
wages for each piece of output.   In America, in particular,
a further advantage has been claimed for the various types of
bonus system, that they reduce the costs incidental to a large
" labour turnover "—to workers leaving their job through
dissatisfaction or in the hope of self-improvement, and seeking
work from another employer : a subject on which something
will be said in a later chapter.

§ 4. **Rate-cutting.** One thing which, more than any other,
has been the ground of trade union opposition to payment
by results has been the occurrence of rate-cutting : namely,
the reduction of the rate at which piece-work is paid after
workers have been put on a piece-work system and have
been induced to increase their speed of work under the attrac-

[1] There may well be an economy even in the circulating capital in
so far as the acceleration of work results (as it will tend to do) in a decrease
of the period of production.   In other words, the increased output of
work will be associated with capital-saving results.   This is an important
qualification of the statement, made in the first edition of this book,
but omitted from later editions, that the tendency of " speed-up " methods
will be to lower piece-rates on the ground that the intensification of work
is equivalent to an increased supply of labour, tending to cheapen its
price.

tion of higher earnings. Even when this occurrence is occasional rather than frequent, it may be sufficient to spread widespread suspicion of the system and provoke opposition to its introduction. The worker naturally regards such cases as evidence that the chief intention of the system is to encourage the worker to increase his pace, and then when this has been achieved to cheat him of increased earnings by scaling down the rate at which he is paid. The employer on his side pleads in defence of his action that it is extraordinarily hard to fix a rate in advance which will turn out to be " economic " for that type of work when higher levels of output have been attained. If the rates are fixed too low in the first place, discontent is likely to arise because the relative earnings of piece-workers and time-workers do not differ enough to remunerate the former for their greater exertions ; while if they are fixed at a level which raises the wage-cost of output, the employer will be faced with the alternative of either reducing the rate subsequently or else dismissing some of his men. This difficulty in the fixation of rates has proved a particular stimulus to the adoption of what are called " time and motion " studies as a basis of rate-fixation. But apart from unavoidable difficulties in fixing the initial rate, there is a reason which may impose on an employer the necessity of subsequently reducing his rate that an individual employer can hardly foresee : namely, a change in the market-price of his product. Indeed, it is highly probable that, if an increase of output resulting from an introduction of piece-rates has become general to a whole industry, a fall in selling-price will occur. How likely this is will depend on whether the demand for the product of the industry is elastic or inelastic (being less probable where the demand is elastic than where it is relatively inelastic) ; and it will also depend on the output-policy of other industries as well as on the financial policy of the country at the time, both of which will determine the movement of purchasing-power and of demand in the community at large. But there remains a sufficiently real danger (apart from any malice aforethought on the part of the employers) of economic circumstances inevitably forcing a cut in the original rates, as soon as the " speed-up " has become at all general in the industry, to provide grounds for suspicion that this may occur, and to cause workers to fear that the system will be twisted to their own detriment unless they have a sufficient share in controlling the fixation of rates. And it is to combat the opposition which this suspicion has aroused that in a number of cases in America firms have had to guarantee that a piece-rate, once introduced, will not be altered for a given length of time.

§ 5. **Premium-Bonus Systems.** The result of an ordinary " straight " system of payment by results, where the worker is paid a straight rate of so much per piece however much he does, is, accordingly, to create a situation where before very long the employer may find it unprofitable to employ so many men unless he can scale down the piece-rates which he has been paying. Such a " cutting " of rates will tend to cause hostility to the whole system among the employees ; and such hostility may defeat the aim of the employer in offering an incentive to faster work. For this and more obvious reasons employers tend to prefer more complicated systems of payment by results under which the reward for increased work starts high, but afterwards does not increase proportionately with the work done. This automatically scales down the rate as individual output increases. These more complicated systems are usually called Premium-Bonus Systems, and are based on a " standard time " for a given job, with a bonus for " time saved ". Under the system which Mr. David Rowan introduced in Glasgow in 1898 a " standard time " is laid down for a given piece of work ; and if the work is done in less time than this, the worker receives a percentage bonus equal to the percentage of time saved. It is to be noted that the wage is calculated in terms of a time-rate, the bonus being calculated as so many hours to be paid for in addition to the hours actually spent on the job. Thus, if the standard time is 10 hours and the work is actually done in 8, the ordinary hourly rate for the 8 hours is paid *plus* a bonus of 20 per cent, which amounts to additional payment for another 1·6 hours. An alternative system introduced by Mr. F. A. Halsey in America in 1890 gave as a bonus a third of the hourly rate for the hours saved on the standard time. Thus, if the standard time was 10 and the work was done in 7 hours, the worker would get paid for the 7 hours *plus* a bonus equal to 1 hour's wage. When this sytem was introduced into England by Messrs. Weir it was altered so as to give a *half* of the hourly rate for the time saved as bonus, and in this form came to be known as the Halsey-Weir System. Of the Rowan and the Halsey Systems the former yields the higher actual rate and greater incentive at the early stages of speeding-up. At the point of a 50 per cent reduction on standard time the two systems are identical, each yielding a 50 per cent increase of earnings for what amounts to a doubling of " standard " output. After this point the actual rate falls away faster under the Rowan than under the Halsey System.

Sometimes collective bonuses have been advocated, and in one or two cases the method has been adopted. This is particularly appropriate where men are working in " gangs " and it is difficult to assess the specific contribution of each man, as for instance with boiler-makers' riveting gangs. An example of it was the Priestman System, introduced by Messrs. Priestman of Hull in 1917. Under this the workers were paid as basis the ordinary time-rate, a group-bonus was given proportional to the amount by which the output of the whole group had been increased beyond a given amount, and this bonus was divided so as to increase each man's wages in the same proportion.

§ 6. "Task-Bonus Systems". A different principle underlies the "task-bonus" systems which were used in America in connection with wider schemes of scientific management. These give a substantial bonus to the workers to attain a certain "task" or standard of efficiency, the bonus being added to the ordinary piece-wage. Under the Gantt System the task is sometimes as severe as a doubling of normal output and the bonus given is about 40 or 50 per cent of the wage. The workers who fail to reach the standard get no extra earnings. This is rather like holding a carrot before the nose of a donkey : the donkey may never reach the carrot, but his progress is nevertheless accelerated. The Emerson System, which is another variety, also lays down a certain "task" ; but the "task" is usually not so severe, being designed for the average worker, and the bonus is equivalently smaller and is graduated according to the nearness which the worker gets to the task. The "carrots" are here smaller and less juicy, but the donkey is given one more frequently.

The Taylor System of Differential Piece-work, however, goes a stage further, and, in contrast to Premium-Bonus Systems, makes the piece-rate at which work is paid actually *rise* as the worker's speed of work increases. For instance, if 6 dozen are done in an hour, the piece-rate may be 1s. per gross ; but if 7 dozen are done in an hour, the rate will be raised to, say, 1s. 1d. per gross. The advantage of this scheme, as claimed by its originator, consists in the fact that it makes the position of the slow worker much worse and that of the quick worker much better than it would be under any alternative scheme, and it consequently tends to drive all slow workers out of the factory and to attract to it all the better workers in the trade. In this way a particular employer may be able to skim off for himself all the cream of the labour market ; and he may profit by staffing his works with a smaller number of men who work more quickly even though he has to pay them at more than the normal rate.   But this is an advantage which *one* employer may obtain or even one industry, but which cannot be gained by all employers at the same time : all of them cannot enjoy only the cream. And if the system were generally adopted the necessity of revising rates in a downward direction would be likely to arise more than in other systems of payment by results.

§ 7. The Bedaux System and Point-rating.   One of the main difficulties associated with piece-rate and bonus systems is the adjustment of rates between different jobs in the same factory.   When men are working on a variety of types of machine or producing different sorts of product, the ease with which output can be increased may vary very widely, in one case involving little and in another case a great deal of physical strain on the worker.   This has always been a crucial problem in the fixation of piece-rates : for example, in the case of coal-hewing, where the ease or difficulty of cutting coal will depend on the hewer's positio n in the mine (whether he is on an easy or a difficult seam) or to-day according as coal-cutting is being done mechanically or by hand.   In the cotton industry the amount of yarn that is spun will vary widely according to the type of " mule " on which the work is being done and the " count " or quality of yarn which is being spun, which determines the amount of " twist " which has to be put on the thread and hence the speed with which the mule-carriage travels outwards in the spinning process : a fact that has been responsible for the very elaborate and complicated systems of piece-rates which have been devised in the cotton industry.

Before the Second World War a good deal was heard of

a bonus method known as the Bedaux System which claimed to have this advantage over other bonus systems : that it provided a method of assessing both the bonus-rate and the standard output between various jobs so as to prevent dissatisfaction from arising about different rates of earnings of workers on different jobs. The system had been first devised in 1911 by a Mr. Charles Bedaux in New York, and it enjoyed some popularity among American employers. In 1926 a company, known as Charles E. Bedaux, Ltd., was registered in London as a subsidiary of the Chas. E. Bedaux Co. of New York, with the object of supplying the technical personnel and advice for its introduction by firms in this country. In the next ten years it was introduced in a considerable number of firms on this side of the Atlantic ; but it cannot be said to have been very popular where it was introduced in this country. Its introduction was notable as being the occasion of a number of strikes on the part of workers ; and in 1932 the Trades Union Congress instituted an enquiry into its operation, which revealed that such unions as had had experience of it in their trades were in nearly every case hostile to it. A well-known authority on labour management declared that it yielded lower hourly earnings than most other American bonus systems.[1] Its general effect apparently was to stimulate an increase of output that was proportionately much greater than the increase of pay that it yielded. Enquiries in America showed that it resulted in increases of production of about 50 per cent on the average and increases of earnings to workers of only about 20 per cent.[2]

Since then a number of adaptations of this system have been worked out, usually referred to as Point-Rating Systems. Their common element is that each job, or unit-part of a job,

[1] Dr. C. H. Northcott, in *Unity*, May, 1932.
[2] *Systems of Wage Payment*, National Industrial Conference Board, pp. 108–9.

is allotted a certain number of points or time-units after what is termed a " time study " of the job by experts, commonly called " rate-fixers ". These points or time-units form the basis for the standard time allotted to a job. In the Bedaux system a " standard minute " was taken as the unit; this was supposed to combine an allowance for actual working time and for a rest-pause after exertion ; and the combination of the two in appropriate proportions was alternatively called a B-unit. A job was then rated at so-many standard minutes or B-units, and a worker was paid a bonus in proportion to the amount of work (measured in these time-units) done in a given period over and above the standard. For example, the standard for a job may be assessed as 20 " standard minutes " ; which is the same as saying that the standard task for each hour of work is three such jobs. The worker is paid the ordinary time-rate for the hour worked ; and if he turns out during the hour more than the 60 standard minutes-worth of work, he gets an equivalent bonus ; this bonus being some proportion (which may be 100 per cent or less) of the time-rate for the extra " standard minutes ". Thus, if in an 8-hour day a worker turns out work that has been rated at 500 " standard minutes ", he will get the ordinary time-rate for the 8 hours ($=$ 480 minutes) worked, plus a bonus equal to the time-rate (or some fraction of it) for the extra 20 minutes.

It can be seen that in principle this is akin to a premium bonus system, in that it also is based on the assessment of a standard time for a job ; only the actual method of calculating the bonus for the extra work done in the time is slightly different (depending as it does on measuring this extra work in time-units, instead of basing the bonus on some relationship between " time saved " and " standard time "). The system is considerably more complicated than most ordinary bonus systems, and it is not always easy for the worker to see how

F

his pay-packet has been calculated. Moreover, since the rating of the jobs in the standard units is done by experts (usually coming in from outside the factory or firm) the fixing of the bonus is less susceptible to collective bargaining than are simpler bonus systems. These two reasons may explain a good deal of the distrust, if not opposition, that such systems have often aroused among workers.

§ 8. **The Field of Payment by Results.** One might well wonder at first sight why it is that payment by results is not universally adopted, seeing that it is apparently of such advantage to employers. But it must be remembered that a system of payment by results is not the only method by which an employer may accelerate the pace of work in his factory. He may, for example, achieve the same result by maintaining a larger staff of foremen and supervisors, and where the work is fairly easy to supervise, and the workers are amenable to the persuasion or pressure of foremen, it may be cheaper for him to extract his greater output by such means. In some cases, indeed, one finds a system of bonuses to foremen proportioned to the results of the whole shop. There are also numerous types of work where payment by results is costly or impracticable to introduce and other cases where its influence on output would be negligibly small. Nor is it true that in all cases it is the employer's interest which favours its adoption, and the workers' interest which opposes and obstructs. True, it is more likely to be in the employer's interest than the workers' for reasons that we have discussed. True, there is a considerable area of industry, most notably in the engineering trades, where fierce battle has waged over the system, the employers urging its extension and the trade unions resisting. But there are also other industries, such as the cotton industry, where the system has been in operation for decades and is accepted without question by operatives and trade unions. There are even certain types of work (of which work on the conveyor system is probably the best example) where it may be in the worker's interest to be paid by results in order that he shall have some compensation for any forcing of the pace which the management may exact through its control over the machine-process. The traditional opposition of trade unions to payment by results has been mainly due to the abuses to which it may open the door; and against the forms of exploitation to which it only too frequently gave rise (as for example under the old sub-contracting system) the trade unions looked to the introduction of time-rates as a protection. The workers' opposition to a new method is usually directed less against the system of payment as such than against the uses to which they fear it may be put. Where trade unions are strong enough to impose safeguards against abuses such as rate-cutting or excessive " speed-up ", opposition to it often disappears; and it is a familiar fact that in the socialized industry of the U.S.S.R. systems of payment by results are widely in use.

Payment by results will clearly be to the greatest advantage of the employer where the rate of work depends primarily on the worker himself and on the speed at which he chooses to go, as for instance a turner at a lathe or a coal-hewer. On the other hand, where the rate of work is mainly governed by the speed of the machinery and the worker does little more than keep pace with the machinery in a series of more or less routine operations, it may not make very much difference to the employer whether he pays by piece or by time. In the Ford works, for instance, the fitters merely attach certain screws and bolts as a continuous travelling carriage passes them, and Mr. Ford consequently prefers to pay everyone by time and not on piece-rates. In such cases, as we have seen, it may be the worker, rather than the employer, who prefers piece-payment, so that if he is " speeded-up " he may get some recompense for the extra strain. In certain types of work quality may be more important than quantity. The worker, if he has a monetary interest in quantity, may speed up his work to the detriment of quality and turn out inferior and " shoddy " work. The employer, it is true, can reject definitely bad work and refuse to count it ; but this leads to conflict and dispute and can usually apply only to the worst cases and will not materially raise the average quality of the work that is turned out. No one would suggest that a gardener should be paid according to the number of geraniums he plants, the *chef* according to the steaks that he grills, the ploughman according to the furrows he drives. It is far from true that every case of low output and high costs is curable by an extension of payment by results. As one writer on the subject has said : " It is being recognized more fully to-day (that) output can be influenced by many factors, of which workers' efforts form but one, and that one possibly not always the most important." [1] Low output may be due to faults of management, to insufficient or intermittent supply of materials, tools, or appliances, to bad co-ordination of different parts of the production process, with resulting delays and congestions, to machinery being unsuitable or out of repair, to the work of the office and the drawing-room being inefficient. Payment by results will not enable the employer to remedy any of these.

Payment by results will be most practicable and easiest to handle where the work is of a standardized character and falls into regular " pieces " which can be easily measured and are the same from week to week. But where the work does not fall into easily measurable " pieces ", or where its character is continually changing, the system will be more complicated to operate, as in a foundry where a large number of different types of casting may be made and these different types change

[1] Powell, *Payment by Results*, p. 57.

from day to day or week to week. It is in these cases that hostility to the system on the part of trade unions is most likely to arise. The aim of a trade union, as we shall see in a later chapter, is to improve the earnings of its members by bargaining *collectively*, or as a group, with the employer over wage-rates. Where the work is standardized and regular, piece-rates as well as time-rates can be fixed by direct bargaining between the trade unions and the employers, the rates for different types of work being drawn up in what is called a " piece-list ", agreed on between the two sides and posted in the workshop. Such " piece-lists " exist in a large number of trades such as the textile and the boot and shoe industries. Even here, of course, certain difficulties of interpretation and consequent disputes may arise in deciding into which of the various categories a particular job may fall ; and in such cases some impartial arbitrator may have to be called in, or as in the cotton industry where the piece-lists are extraordinarily complicated the employers may decide to leave the decision to trade union officials, who in this case are specially appointed for the purpose. But where the work is very varied in character and new types of work are continually arising, standardized piece-lists are not possible and piece-rates have to be settled for each job separately by a direct bargain between the management and the individual worker. The fact that in the engineering trades piece-rates have been fixed traditionally in this way by what is known as the method of " mutuality," instead of by piece-lists collectively negotiated and agreed upon, is apparently in the main responsible for the greater opposition that has in the past been put up by the engineering trade unions to the extension of payment by results than in other trades. During the War the difficulty became particularly great owing to the large number of new types of work that were being continually introduced, and owing to the wholesale promotion of unskilled men on to skilled jobs (known as "dilution"). In each case a new bargain had to be made as to the rate between the worker concerned and the management; and it was in order to introduce an element of "collective bargaining" into the settlement of such rates that the custom spread in the engineering and furnishing trades for the workers in each shop to elect a shop steward who should act as their spokesman to the management, and for the various shop stewards in turn to come together in a works committee. Between the two wars, however, there was a big extension of standardized work in engineering, with increased use of automatic machinery, and the field for payment by results was greatly extended as a result. Where cases arise in which it is not possible for a trade union to fix piece-rates by collective bargaining, it is now fairly common to exact a safeguarding condition that piece-workers shall not earn less than the prevailing time-rate. This is done in the engineering trades. Frequently it is urged that piece-workers should be guaranteed more than the normal time-rate, namely, "time-and-a-quarter", or "time-and-a-third", since men on piece-rates usually work at a greater intensity than time-workers, and the former may be suffering an injustice if they are receiving no more than the latter while in practice doing more work.

§ 9. Sub-contracting. In cases where the workers are weak and unorganized a system of payment by results may hold the door open to numerous methods of exploitation, if only for the reason that where the method of payment is more complicated, and where it is such as to encourage the worker to accelerate his speed of work, there is more chance of advantage being taken of the worker's ignorance and weakness. In the old days abuses of this kind attached particularly to a system known as "sub-contracting" which was then fairly common. Under this system, which was really a survival from the Domestic System before the coming of factories, the capitalist would give out work at a certain price to a small man or gang-master or sub-contractor, who then, in turn, employed workmen on the job. The sub-contractor secured his profit by getting the work done at less than the price at which he had contracted with his employer ; and as a result he had a special inducement to reduce the wages he paid to a minimum. If the employer " beat him down ", he in turn would " beat down " the wage he paid to those he employed. The working of a mine was often given over at a price to a " butty ", as he was called. In the tin mines of Cornwall the working of a mine was often let out to a " gang-master " on what was called " tut-work " by a process of " Dutch Auction ", under which the price started high and the job finally went to the lowest bidder. In the middle of the nineteenth century a large amount of the work of railway construction was done on a basis of sub-contract. To-day there are still certain survivals of this. In the Midlands coal-field the " butty " still survives in the shape of the hewer who gets a certain " stall " allotted to him when a coal seam is opened up at a certain price per ton for the coal he sends out from his " stall ". He, in turn, employs assistants, often at day-rates and not piece-rates, to help him in working the " stall ". But to-day the rates both of the " butty " and his assistants are as a rule regulated by trade union agreements ; although apparently there is not infrequently some " oiling of the palm " to secure the allotment of the most favourable " stalls ". The system also survives in a large number of the small hand trades, such as the clothing trades, where work is given out on a sub-contract basis, and it is here that some of the worst cases of " sweating " are generally found. The economist McCulloch once praised the sub-contract system in flamboyant terms. " It is in truth," he said, " the broadest, the easiest, and the safest of the various channels by which diligent, sagacious and frugal individuals emerge from poverty and attain to respectability and opulence. Those who thus rise to distinction may be emphatically said to be the architects of their own fortunes. They owe nothing to interest, to favour or to any unworthy means." But to-day it is generally recognized that the system is bad unless carefully hedged with numerous safeguards. As trade unions have developed they have usually been hostile to the system and in their original attacks on it turned towards time-rates as providing a safeguard against its numerous abuses.

§ 10. **Weighing and Measuring.** There are two particular ways in which a piece-worker, unsupported by legal safeguards or by a trade union, may be an easy victim for an employer or sub-contractor or foreman who is ready to take advantage of the weakness of an employee. The worker may have undertaken work on a verbal understanding as to the rate. When pay-day comes he may find that his pay has been calculated at a lower rate. Or, again, he may find that in the weighing or the counting of his work he has been credited with a smaller quantity than he thinks that he has really done. It is his word against his employer's ; and if the employer sticks to his point, the worker has no evidence that he is right and no redress. If the worker throws up the job, the employer can probably get another quite easily to fill his place ; and if the vacancy cannot be filled quickly the employer loses only a little profit, whereas the worker fears that he may fare no better elsewhere and that he may be unable to get other work at all. Frequently more subtle issues may arise over the precise character or quality of the work that was ordered or over the interpretation of " bad work ".

To deal with this a whole series of Acts of Parliament has been passed. As far back as 1824 an Act provided for the use of a " ticket " to be given out to the worker with each piece of work, stating the character of the work to be done and the piece-rate to be paid for it. This " ticket " was to constitute legal evidence in any dispute, but its use remained optional for an employer. In 1845, the use of " tickets " was made compulsory in the hosiery trade and in silk weaving, where there had been much complaint of abuses in this respect. The Factory and Workshop Act of 1891 made the giving of written particulars of work compulsory in all textile factories ; in 1895 the Home Secretary was empowered to extend this obligation by special order to other trades; and in 1901 it was made generally compulsory for employers in giving out piece-work either to post a list of rates in a prominent place or else to issue a " ticket " of particulars with each piece of work. With regard to the measuring or weighing of the work done, the miners in 1872 secured the right of appointing a " check-weigher " elected by the piece-workers in a mine and paid by them to represent the men when the weighing of tubs was taking place at the pit-head. But this nominal right was only a beginning : there were ways in which a mine manager could hoodwink the " interfering " check-weigher, if he desired, or even exert pressure upon his election. Later legislation, accordingly, provided that the check-weigher's rights should be actual as well as nominal. He was to have " every facility afforded to him for enabling him to fulfil the duties for which he is stationed ", while on the other hand it was made illegal for him to impede the working of the mine or to interfere with the weighing. By an Act of 1894 it was made an offence for an owner or manager to exert " improper influence " on the election of a check-weigher, whether by threats, bribes or dismissal, or to refuse to give facilities for such an election. Finally the Act of 1919 provided for an extension of the system to other industries—to iron and steel founding, casting and rolling, to the loading and unloading of vessels, to chalk and limestone quarrying, and to cement and lime-working. The Home Secretary was further empowered to extend the system to any other trade that he thought fit. An important new clause in this latest Act made it necessary for the employer to give " reasonable notice " to the check-weigher of the time and place at which the weighing was to take place.

§ 11. Truck and Deductions.

Another respect in which advantage may be taken of the weakness of an unorganized worker is in various kinds of deductions from his wages. These deductions may take the form of fines for bad work or bad time-keeping or indiscipline, or they may be on account of materials or tools supplied. Where the employer owns a shop or a canteen, runs a benefit club, or rents a house to his employees, he may deduct the value of what is purchased at the shop, or the club fees, or the rent of the house, from the wages that are paid, handing over only the balance in actual cash. In the early factory towns this practice was quite common, gaining the name of the Truck System, and frequently resulting in considerable evil and abuse. Sometimes the employer would pay the worker entirely in kind, instead of cash ; and if the foodstuffs in question were of poor quality, were of little use to him, or were of less value than the wage he had contracted for, the worker had seldom any redress. In other cases the employer might pay part of his wages, not in cash, but in vouchers or orders on a neighbouring " tommy-shop ", as it was called, owned by himself or a confederate ; and if at this shop the worker was charged exorbitant prices or given shoddy goods, he had no freedom to go elsewhere unless he abandoned his employment. Since the middle of the eighteenth century legislation had been in force providing that wages should only be paid " in good and lawful money of the kingdom " ; but the legislation remained a dead letter. The first serious attempt to deal with the evil was the Truck Act of 1831. This prohibited any contract which made the worker agree to take his wages in any other form than cash, or bound him to spend his wages in any particular way, and forbade deductions from wages on account of fines. A later Act in 1887 prohibited entirely the payment of wages in the form of orders for goods on tradesmen, and made it illegal for a master to dismiss an employee because he did not spend his money in a particular way. The matter of deductions from wages for fines and tools, etc., was finally dealt with in the Truck Act of 1896. This Act, in distinction from that of 1831, legalized certain deductions of this kind, provided that notice was given and displayed publicly of the items for which such deductions would be made. The position, therefore, as it exists to-day, is that payment of wages in any other form than cash is illegal, as is also any compulsion on the worker as to the way in which he spends his wages. It is also illegal (by the Shop Club Act of 1902) for an employer to make it a condition of employment that the worker should join any particular " shop club " or friendly society or private benefit club of his own. On the other hand, deductions from wages on account of rents, of tools and materials supplied, and of disciplinary fines are allowed. In some of these instances there still remains room, therefore, for an employer who desires to " nibble " by indirect means at the wages he pays to do so ; and the extent and character of such deductions remain a subject at times for disagreements and disputes.

§ 12. **Profit-sharing.** Some employers, in addition to, or instead of, ordinary systems of payment by results, favour a system known as profit-sharing with the aim of stimulating a collective spirit among the work-people favourable to greater output, and of giving to the employees a financial interest in the success of the firm. Sometimes the system is coupled

with some co-partnership scheme under which the employees
are given special facilities for taking up shares in the business
and are given a small degree of representation on the Board.
Not infrequently a further advantage is hoped for from the
scheme in detaching the workers from a trade union and
freeing the management from the constriction of collective
bargaining and possible strikes. An early instance of this
was a scheme introduced by Henry Briggs, Son & Co., colliery
owners of Normanton, in 1865, together with special share-
holding privileges and a seat on the Board of Directors for
a workers' representative. A condition was made, however,
that in order to receive the profit-bonus the employees must
abandon membership of any trade union ; and when later
a strike was declared against a wage-reduction the bonus was
discontinued. In this case the right of the men to receive
the bonus was not legally established, but rested at the will
of the shareholders. Messrs. Fox, Head & Co., iron manufacturers of Middlesbrough, introduced a similar scheme in
1866. Fifteen years previously in France the *Compagnie
d'Assurances Générales* had introduced an interesting form of
deferred profit-sharing with the express object of preventing
other firms from drawing away its best employees by offers
of a higher salary. This profit-bonus was not paid out immediately, but was accumulated in a Provident Fund and then
paid in an accumulated bonus to every employee of 25 years
standing or over 65 years of age. A more recent instance in
England is the well-known scheme of the South Metropolitan
Gas Company, introduced in 1889, as an inducement to
terminate a strike, and containing originally a condition that
those participating in the scheme should not be members
of a trade union—a condition which was later abandoned.

The ground covered by such schemes in this country is not
very wide, although there was some increase after the First
World War. In 1936 there were 412 schemes in operation

covering 260,000 employees.   On the average the profit-bonus
amounted to some 5–6 per cent of the worker's wage, and seldom exceeded in all 10 per cent of the total profits.   About
another 400 schemes had also been started at one time or
another and subsequently terminated.   An advantage frequently cited for the system is that it implies the imparting of
information concerning profits to the workers.   But apart
from this, profit-sharing seems to amount to little more than a
particular form of bonus system of wage-payment—a collective
bonus assessed, not according to the results of a particular
workman or a gang of workmen, but according to the financial
results of the whole concern.   In some respects it is less likely
to achieve its desired results than other bonus systems of payment, since the bonus is less directly related to the worker's
own effort, and is consequently likely to act as a weaker
incentive to him to increase his exertions, depending as it
does on several factors outside the workers' control, such as
financial circumstances, the state of the market and the
efficiency of the management.   In so far as it is successful in
its aim it will be successful for precisely the same reason as
is any other bonus system—for the reason that it increases
the intensity of work and the productivity of labour, and so
increases gross product to a greater extent than the bonus
which had to be paid away.   But trade unions have generally
had the suspicion that there was an additional aim in such
schemes : namely, to attach the worker more closely to a particular firm and so to free the employer from the restraints of a
collective bargain by sapping the strength of trade unionism.
And it is because they suspect such an aim to be present in
most profit-sharing schemes, explicit or implicit, that the tradition of trade unionism has been hostile to such proposals.

§ 13. Payment by Results and Earnings.   In all methods of
payment the actual results which they yield will vary as much

with the circumstances in which they are introduced as with the particular method adopted. Hence it is the circumstances surrounding them rather than the method itself on which we must fix our attention in judging what the effect will be upon the interests of employers and employed : and it is difficult to say that any one system is itself good or bad irrespective of the circumstances in which it is adopted. One may, of course, classify different methods according to how they relate changes in pay to changes in effort. But this is not enough unless one knows what the basic rate is at which men are being paid. For example, in judging whether a piece-rate is of benefit to a worker, it is not sufficient to know that it gives him a 10 per cent increase in wage for a 10 per cent increase of effort. If the initial wage is low relatively to the effort involved, the worker may be getting only a few pence extra for increasing his labour and his output by a large amount, and a piece-worker working at a quarter or a third as fast again as time-workers may be earning little more than the latter obtain. In the case of Premium-Bonus Systems everything will depend on the " standard-time " that is set. If the standard is set severely at the speed of the fastest man, only a few will achieve the task in less time and only a few will enjoy the bonus. Even though the wage may increase proportionately for increased work in excess of the *standard*, the ratio of increased pay to increased effort may be small compared with the *normal* output of an average worker if the standard set is a high one. Similarly with profit-sharing, the basic wage which the worker receives is probably more important than the amount of the additional profit-bonus he gets. If an employer pays £10 a year to each man as bonus, but at the same time manages to reduce wages by 4s. a week all round, his total wages-bill will be no greater than before and the scheme will be costing him nothing. This is why a trade union may be more concerned with the effect of a new method on collective bargaining than with its immediate promise of higher earnings, and why the workers may be more hostile to payment by results when they are weakly organized than when they feel they are in a strong enough position to control the manner of its operation.

To avoid misunderstanding, it should be remembered that few systems of piece-rates are in practice unrelated to a standard of earnings per unit of time. In other words, piece-rates usually operate within a kind of framework of time earnings ; and many of the complications that are met with in the actual operation of these systems is due to the fact that various sorts of compromise are attempted between maintaining *uniform rates* per quantity of output in all conditions and places and *uniform earnings* per period of time. For example, the national wage agreement in the boot and shoe industry does not run in terms of job-prices at all. It merely stipulates certain weekly rates of earnings for workers of various categories, and then directs that piece-rates shall be so fixed in each locality " as to give to the average operative an earning capacity of 25 per cent over " the rates of earnings laid down. This implies that piece-rates shall always be adjusted in order to yield uniform earnings, so far as an " average operative " is concerned. Certain exceptions are made to this in jobs " where exceptional skill or length of training are required " or " in outlying districts " where goods of lower quality are being made. The local interpretation, however, of this uniform-earnings policy varies considerably. In some centres, such as Northampton, piece-prices for the job are fixed separately for each firm ; [1] with the result that

---

[1] These so-called " Shop Statements " apply to the closing, making and finishing departments ; but in the clicking and rough-stuff departments there are District Statements, with uniform prices for the whole district, which are graded according to the type of operation, of shoe and of material used.

the better organized and equipped firm has lower wage-costs per shoe than the less efficient firm, since the piece-prices will tend to be adjusted downwards in the case of the former to allow for the fact that better organization and machinery enable the operative to get through more pieces in a day. In other centres, however (e.g. Norwich and Leicester), there are uniform price-lists for jobs applicable to all (or nearly all) firms; so that wage-costs are thereby made uniform between firms, whereas workers in a more efficient firm will tend to have higher earnings than those employed in a less efficient one. To deal with the complicating factor of differing machine-speeds, and their effects on output-rates and earnings, there has been some opinion in the industry in favour of establishing uniform machine-prices nationally : i.e. the same piece-price for work done on the same machine in all manufacturing districts.

The matter of adjusting piece-rates to differing machine-speeds, so as not to depart too far from a uniform-earnings system and to give some advantage in costs to the firm introducing improved machinery, has been responsible for much of the complications of piece-rate systems in the textile industry. In cotton-spinning the amount of yarn spun in a given time varies both with the quality of yarn spun (the amount of " twist " it receives in the spinning process) and according to the newness or oldness of the machinery. One traditional system (the so-called Bolton List) made allowance for changes in the amount of yarn spun due to the *first* of these reasons, but not for changes due to the second of them. Another (the so-called Oldham List) provided for automatic adjustment in the price paid to the operative per length of yarn spun according as the speed of spinning varied for *either* of these reasons, thereby approximating to a uniform-earnings arrangement.[1] Hence, improvements in machinery in the

[1] With the exception that the results of larger output due to increased

course of time have had different effects both on costs and
on earnings in different firms according to the system of piece-
rates under which they have been working. A similar contrast
exists between the main price-list that has operated in the
past over a large part of the North Lancashire cotton-weaving
district (the N. Lancs. Cotton Weaving List) and that which
prevailed over a large section of woollen weaving in Yorkshire
(the Huddersfield Weaving List) : in the latter provision was
made, and in the former it was not made, for piece-prices to
fall as improvements in machinery increased the speed of
weaving.[1] The precise effects of a system of wage-payment
on workers' earnings cannot, therefore, be estimated until
details such as these are fully taken into account.

§ 14. Sliding-scales. In a number of industries wage-agreements provide that the money rates of wages agreed upon
shall be attached to a certain index according to a sliding-
scale, and made to vary from time to time according to variations in this index. The three main types of sliding-scale
in operation are those attached respectively to the cost of
living index number, to the price of the product of the in-
pustry in question and to some index of the profits of the
industry. Profit-sharing, of which we have already spoken,

machinery-speed was divided half-and-half between lower costs to the
employer and higher earnings to the operative ; and that as regards
mule-length (i.e. number of spindles per mule, which affects the amount
of work required of the minder) two-thirds of the effect of extra output
due to extra length accrued in extra earnings.
    [1] It has been estimated that between 1886 and 1913, although wage-
rates in cotton-weaving only rose by about 18 per cent, the rate of earnings probably increased by twice as much owing to improvements in
machinery and faster weaving. On the other hand, between the wars
it is probable that machinery deteriorated, while inferior materials and
departures from specialization slowed-up output, so that weavers' earnings fell for these reasons. This, combined with poor wage-rates and
under-employment, made hourly earnings of weavers in the 1930's almost
the lowest of any trade for male workers.

G

can be said to be a variety of the third type, with this difference :
that it is the profits of the single firm according to which the
wage-bonus is assessed, and not the profits of a whole industry.
An important example of the profit-sliding-scale was the
system of wage-ascertainments introduced by the 1921
agreement into the coal-mining industry. Here, the gross
receipts of the industry, after the deduction first of costs
other than wages, and then of what are termed " standard
wages " and " standard profits ", were divided between wages
and profits in certain proportions, with the intention that
wages and profits should move up or down with the total
receipts of the industry.[1] The calculation, however, was
made separately in each colliery district, with the result that
the level and the movement of wages might be very different
in South Wales or Durham or Fifeshire from what it was in
Lancashire or Derbyshire or Yorkshire. The chief example
to-day of the sliding-scale based on the selling-price of the
product is in iron and steel ; but in the past its introduction
was often the occasion for strenuous opposition from the
workers and for strikes against the system. This was the
case at the end of last century in certain colliery districts in
the north, where the sliding-scale was introduced, and fierce
struggles took place over a number of years which finally
resulted in its withdrawal. As a bone of contention it even
divided the trade union world, the unions in the older colliery
districts of Northumberland and Durham (also South Wales)
supporting it, and the newer unions in Yorkshire and Lancashire opposing it and breaking away to form a new national

---

[1] This distribution of receipts between profits and wages was, however,
subject to the payment of a certain minimum amount to wage-earners.
If in any year these receipts were insufficient to pay this minimum, the
employers had to forgo some of their standard profits, but the deficiency
was carried forward to subsequent years as a first charge on any surplus.
In most years between the wars there was such a deficiency and wages
were down on the minimum.

federation. The sliding-scale based on the cost of living index is the most common of the three, and is in operation in a number of industries including railways, hosiery, and the boot and shoe trade. Certain Wages Councils [1] attach such a sliding-scale to the minimum wage-rates which they lay down, so that the minimum rates in operation automatically move up or down by some fraction of a penny for every so many points by which the cost of living index number of the Ministry of Labour changes.

It is to be noticed that a sliding-scale has this fundamental difference from any of the systems of payment which we have been discussing. It is in no way concerned with the *basis* on which work is paid : whether it is paid on a piece-basis or a time-basis or how the pay is made to vary with length of time or quantity of output. It is solely concerned with *changes* in the rate (on whatever basis or at whatever level this is fixed), according as certain other features in the economic situation change in the course of time. The intention is to make wages more flexible and to allow for their automatic readjustment when there is some change of circumstances which, it is considered, makes this readjustment necessary. It is important to notice, however, that in their pursuit of flexibility these sliding-scales follow different intentions. The sliding-scales based on profits or on selling-price are designed to cause wages to vary according as the prosperity of the industry varies, taking profit and selling-price respectively as indices of this prosperity. As servant of this intention the selling-price scale has the evident weakness that by itself it is no true indicator of the state of trade : a fall in selling-price may be an indication equally well of the fall in cost of some important raw material or of greater economy in the use of machinery as of a decline in the market demand for the product. A complaint made against the coal sliding-scale last

[1] See Chapter VIII below.

century was that wages during bad times seemed to have
"no bottom", since it encouraged competitive undercutting
of coal-prices to an excessive extent by giving an additional
incentive (that of lower wages) to employers to reduce the
price of coal. To some extent this latter difficulty may
apply also to the profit sliding-scale; although in other
respects (apart from certain practical difficulties of its own,
chiefly concerned with the calculation of profits) it is more
successful in fulfilling its intention. The cost of living scale,
on the other hand, must clearly be judged by some other
criterion. As an index of the state of prosperity in a particular industry it is clearly useless, since it is based on the
cost of purchasing a variety of articles in which neither the
product nor any of the materials of the industry in question
may be included. Only by coincidence is the movement of
this index likely to correspond with movements in either the
market-price or the profits of the industry in question. What
the cost of living scale achieves is an approximate stability
in *real* wages for the duration of a wage-agreement. This
may not suit the requirements of the employers in a particular
industry, if they desire to adapt wage-rates to changing trade
conditions. But if the intention of a trade union or a
minimum-wage authority in making a wage-agreement is to
determine a certain level of real wages, rather than of money
wages, then this type of scale can be said best to fulfil their
intention. There is also this which is often said in defence
of a cost of living scale : when large movements in the general
price-level take place, the prices of most things are likely to
move in the same *direction*, if not in the same degree ; and
accordingly this scale, while it secures to the worker a stable
real wage, at the same time causes the *money* wage to be
more flexible than would otherwise be the case, and flexible
in the same direction as the movements of other prices. The
crucial question remains, however, whether flexibility of this

kind is a desirable aim to pursue : whether if money-wages are adapted to changing conditions of trade, this diminishes the unemployment which occurs in depression, or whether a fluctuation of economic conditions is steadied by the presence of a constant element in the situation (rigid money wages).

§ 15. Hours of Work. Formerly employers devoted more attention to increasing output by the extension of hours than to increasing the intensity of the work done in each hour ; and a hundred years ago it was quite common for hours of work to be over 12 and even to reach 16 hours a day. In doing this, employers neglected the fact that there was such a thing as an " economy of shorter hours " as well as of higher wages, and that in lengthening hours they were ultimately defeating their own ends, since the fatigue of longer hours affected the health and efficiency of workers and undermined their ability to maintain any high intensity of work.   Like the " economy of higher wages ", the economy of shorter hours only operates, of course, up to a point. As hours are reduced, the increase in output per hour will at first tend to be in greater proportion than the reduction of hours, as a consequence of the higher intensity of work per hour that results.   But a point will come where the proportionate increase in hourly output is no longer greater than the proportionate reduction of hours ; and it will be at this point that the employer finds his total output at a maximum. There has been some controversy as to where this point comes, some placing it as low as 6 working hours per day, others placing it at 9 hours or somewhat more.   A considerable body of evidence exists to suggest that in a number of occupations it stands at about 8 hours, with variations below and above this figure for different trades according to the type of work ; and it seems fairly certain that in most trades any extension beyond 9 hours would lower and not increase the

total daily or weekly output. This was shown with particular
force during the First World War when in the munitions
trades hours were increased and holidays cut down in the
attempt to increase output. But it was quickly realized that
this method of increasing output was defeating its own end ;
and a reversion took place to shorter hours of working.
This is, of course, to speak only of the effect of changed
hours on output, which is what interests the employer. It
is not to say that it might not be socially desirable to shorten
hours beyond this point, in view of the advantage of greater
leisure and less fatigue.

In recent decades, accordingly, employers have found it in
their interest to devote their attention to the intensive speeding-
up of work instead of to lengthening hours ; although this,
too, has its limits, where the heightened pace of work reacts
through fatigue on efficiency. As a result employers have
not been unwilling on the whole to accede to the trade union
demand for shorter working hours ; and to-day in the majority
of trades the normal working hours per week are limited by
collective agreement between trade unions and employers to
44 or 45 hours. If a worker is employed for longer than this,
he has to be paid for the extra hours at a specially high
" overtime " rate, which acts as a deterrent to the management from working its men longer than the normal period.
In certain cases, as in the building trade, it is part of the
agreement that a particular employer who wishes to work
" overtime " shall first obtain the consent of the local trade
union secretary. It is usual when a trade union secures a
reduction of hours for it to insist on a raising of the hourly
rates so that weekly earnings do not fall as a result of the
shortening of hours. This takes away from the employer
much of the advantage which shortened hours yield. But,
if the result is an increased output per hour, it is clearly
equitable that hourly wage-rates should be equivalently raised.

Apart from legislating in the interest of women and children, the State has taken little part in limiting the hours of labour ; although in most cases where men and women are employed in the same factory a limitation on the hours of the latter has automatically limited also the hours which the former can work. The exception is that of coal-mining, where hours underground were limited by law in 1908 to 8 hours, and to 7 hours in 1919 ; although the limit was subsequently raised again to 7½ hours. Shop assistants have also been legislated for in the Shop-closing Acts. But apart from this, legal limitation on the hours of male workers has not been introduced in this country ; and while an international convention to limit hours by law to 48 per week was adopted at the Washington Conference in 1920, the British Government subsequently decided not to carry it into effect. The shortening of working hours that has occurred over the last half-century has been the product of collective bargaining between trade unions and employers and is embodied in collective agreements between the two sides.

CHAPTER IV

THEORIES OF WAGES

§ 1. What a Theory of Wages tries to do. When an economist constructs a theory of wages, what he is trying to do is to sketch an abstract picture or diagram of the way in which wages, as the price of labour-power, are connected with other prices and other economic quantities. He is sketching a picture made up of relationships of interdependence of such a kind that a change taking place at any one point produces related shifts and changes over the whole of the area that he is studying. His picture is a true portrait or not according as its contours correspond or do not correspond to the contours of the real world which it claims to depict. At the same time he generally tries to do something more than draw a picture. Not only does he attempt to simplify the picture in greater or less degree, so as to emphasize those relationships which he thinks to be of major importance ; but he tries to depict them in such a way as to rest the structure of interdependent relationships on certain " key " quantities, whose position can be known independently of the rest, and which, when known, are sufficient to enable him to calculate the position of the other variable quantities (in this case wages). Of course, in actuality nothing is independent and everything reacts in some degree on everything else. But if this one-way influence of the " key " factors on the other variable quantities is a sufficiently dominant one, contrary influences can be treated as negligible and the assumption of independence can be taken as " good enough " for most purposes. One will then have a theory which enables one to calculate, or to determine, what the wage-level must be as soon as these given data, or key factors, are known; just as in mechanics a theorem enables one to postulate a certain equilibrium-position or certain paths of movements, given the position and strength of the determining forces. The theory will also tell one, in the case of, say, a difference in wages between two periods of time or two countries, to what this difference must be ultimately traceable, in the sense that changes in certain quantities are alone adequate to make possible any permanent changes in wages. The theory (in so far as it is true) starts from a description of how things are actually interconnected as basis for a calculation of what changes will occur in certain situations. In turn, such calculations can be used as a guide to action—to show how things can be changed.

But a theory may be untrue because the connections which it depicts do not give a true picture of the real world, either because they are non-existent or because relationships are omitted that are of major importance and have to be taken into account. A theory, again, while true within limits, may not be adequate for the purposes which it is designed to serve —to answer the questions it claims to answer—because the " key " factors which it has singled out as basis of its calculations and forecasts are in fact much less independent of the other variable quantities than it has supposed. People have sometimes said of theories of wages that the labour-market is in fact much too complex a tangle of interacting forces for any simplified theory to yield calculations which have much validity outside a special type of situation or a limited period of time. Hitherto progress has been hampered by the scarcity of statistical evidence, or even of systematized data, as to how wages actually behave, and how movements of wages are correlated with changes in other factors. Theories of wages have, therefore, had to be built out of a highly simplified picture of the real world, sketching only the broad outlines of the more obvious features, on the basis of general knowledge or else of inference as to the general shape which things have. The paucity of statistical data is to-day beginning to be repaired, and recently some valuable studies have been made of such data, which enable us to fill out our picture in important places. But even here the complexities of the real world are often a serious limitation : variation and change may be sufficiently great for any general statement based upon data drawn from one place or one period of time to have a very limited application to a different place or a later period of time when the situation has altered and the constellation of forces is in significant respects different.

§ 2. **Traditional Theories of Wages.** Traditional theories of wages have been mainly of a fairly rigid kind : that is, they have given a fairly simple and definite statement of the factors which determine the level of wages. Most of them (though not all) have implied that the level of wages cannot, save in rather exceptional cases, be permanently altered (at least, without corresponding damage to wage-earners in some such form as unemployment) by interferences with the free play of economic forces in the labour-market, whether this interference takes the form of trade union action to compel employers to employ men at a certain standard wage or of legislative action by the State to impose a minimum wage. From time to time criticism has been levelled against such theories on the ground that they neglect a number of important relationships (specially a reflex-influence of the wage-level on the given factors) and assume that wages are much more rigidly determined by the given factors which these theories emphasize than is really the case ; and in recent years such criticism has again gathered force and accumulated some weighty arguments in its train. Consideration of this discussion will be deferred to the next chapter. For the moment we are concerned with what the traditional theories have

themselves maintained. These theories can be broadly classi-
fied into two main types, according to the type of determining
factor on which their emphasis has rested. On the one hand
are those theories which have explained wages predominantly
in terms of factors which influence the *supply* of labour-power
—virtually, cost of production theories of wages. On the
other hand are those theories which have treated wages as
being determined primarily by certain factors which influence
employers' *demand* for labour, such as the supply of capital
and/or the productivity of labour. Some economists (most
notably, Marshall [1]) have tried to erect a synthesis of the two
types of explanation and to hold a balance between the two
sets of determining influence ; and so have produced a theory
of a hybrid type.

§ 3. **The Subsistence Theory.** The earliest theory that we
meet was a supply-theory and was in some ways the simplest
of them all. It stated simply that the price of labour depended
on the subsistence of the labourer. Wages equalled the
amount of commodities necessary to feed and clothe a worker
and his family, which represented the cost to society of
" enabling the labourers to subsist and to perpetuate their
race " (Ricardo). This implied that what the worker received
under a wage-system was the same as what he received under
slavery or serfdom—in each case enough to cover the labourer's
" wear and tear ". Indeed, some writers followed Adam
Smith in thinking that " though the wear and tear of a free
servant is equally at the expense of his master, it generally
costs him much less than that of a slave ", because the free
labourer would be more frugal and economical in arranging
his own diet than would an overseer who managed the feeding
of the slaves. At the same time the labour of a free labourer

---

[1] Marshall's theory was also less rigid, and allowed more scope for the
action of trade unions than did the theories of many other economists.

would probably be more efficient and productive. It followed that if the price of necessaries increased or decreased, money wages also would be bound to rise or fall before very long; and if a tax was imposed on wages, wages must rise by an equivalent amount and the burden of the tax in this way be thrown upon the employer.

This theory relied for its validity on the famous Malthusian law of population, which was widely accepted by economists and others at the beginning of the nineteenth century. In the language of later economists, it implied that the supply of labour was infinitely elastic : that this supply would always be increased indefinitely if the price offered for it rose above a certain level. If wages rose above what was necessary to maintain the supply of labour, then workers would have larger families and the labour supply would increase. With an increased labour supply there would be more competition for the employment available, so that wages as a result would inevitably fall again. Conversely, if wages fell below the subsistence level, children would die off or never be born, and this would result in a decreased labour supply in the next generation, so that the competition of masters for the smaller number of workers would raise wages again. It was a case of mechanical equilibrium : like the pendulum of a clock, any disturbance from the " normal " position brought into play forces which would bring it back to " normal " again. Things might take some time to settle down in the equilibrium—" market price " for some time might fluctuate about " normal price "—but given sufficient time the equilibrium would be restored.

It seems not unlikely that in an early stage of a wage-system this law approximately holds. But it probably holds rather because of the continual inflow of new labour from the countryside to seek employment in the towns, as the result of village poverty, enclosures, agricultural changes and

destruction of handicrafts, than of any " natural " law governing the growth of population and continually keeping wages
from rising above subsistence. In the light of modern experience there is certainly no warrant for assuming that population
will automatically increase as wages rise: in fact, there is
some evidence that the contrary is the case. But here again
the alleged connection between wages and population may
be nearer to the truth when applied to workers on a very low
standard of life, who because of their poverty are improvident
of the future and whose families are only precluded from
increase because their children die of malnutrition.

§ 4. **The Influence of Habit and Custom.** But the exponents of
this Subsistence Theory themselves made one admission which
really undermined their theory as a complete explanation of
wages. Ricardo, for instance, maintained that habit and
custom were instrumental in determining what was " necessary " in the workers' diet. In the subsistence level to which
wages were supposed to adapt themselves was included, not
only bare physical necessities, but also a modicum of comforts as well. The reason for this, although not very clearly
stated, was apparently a double one. The worker, having
grown accustomed to certain small comforts such as a glass of
ale and a pipe of tobacco, would dispense with physical
necessities rather than with these, if his wages were reduced.
Habit, in other words, turned these comforts into " conventional necessities ". Moreover, in so far as the worker made
any economic calculations in deciding when it was politic to
marry and how large a family it was safe to have, it was clearly
the standard of life which he *thought* to be necessary that
entered into his decision.

To admit a variable quantity such as habit as being important was to make an appreciable hole in the completeness
of the theory. It meant that the subsistence theory in its

absolute form only held good so long as one could take habit and custom for granted and assume a certain level of conventional necessaries as entering into the subsistence level. But since habits change, this meant that the theory could only be applied to a limited period of time over which habit and custom could be assumed to be constant : it was not competent to sustain long-term forecasts over a period during which custom might change appreciably. Moreover, a change of wage might itself be the *cause* of a change of habit, since a new wage-level accustomed wage-earners to a new standard. In this case the causal influence would be reversed ; and instead of wages inevitably being made to conform to a subsistence-level by inexorable changes in the supply of labour, the wage-level itself might react on the supply-conditions of labour, and a rise in wages create the very change of conditions which enabled it to be maintained.

It seems clear that Ricardo did not treat this qualification as being of major importance because he regarded the influence of habit as being generally confined to a comparatively short run (a decade or two at most) and considered the law of population—its tendency always to increase up to the limits of subsistence—as sufficiently powerful to assert itself in the long run and to override the influence of any intervening change in habit. For a time the wage-level might show a rising tendency (just as at other times it might stand for some time at less than the bare subsistence-level). This would occur when economic progress was rapid, when capital was continually accumulating and industry expanding, so that the demand for labour was increasing faster than the supply. As wages rose, new habits would be formed in the working class, introducing new comforts into their standard of life ; and at such periods " the condition of the labourer is flourishing and happy (and) he has it in his power to command a greater proportion of the necessaries and enjoyments of life

and therefore to rear a healthy and numerous family ". But
the inexorable pressure of human procreativeness was ever
fast on the heels of this improvement ; and so soon as economic progress slackened, the conditions favourable to a rise
in wages would tend to come to an end : the supply of labour
would catch up the demand ; and once the wage-level had
started to fall again, habit would be revised as easily in a
downward direction as it had previously been in an upward
direction.

It is not altogether clear whether Ricardo thought that the
law of population would generally suffice to produce such a
relapse, even while economic progress continued ; or whether
he treated the subsistence theory as a " static " theory, pos-
tulating the equilibrium-level to which wages would return
when, after a period of change, progress slowed down to a
standstill. While his statement that " the market rate (of
wages) may, in an improving society, for an indefinite period,
be constantly above " the subsistence-level suggests the latter,
his emphasis on the tendency for the cost of subsistence
itself to rise in a well-populated country suggests the former.
The difference is like the difference in a game of musical
chairs between the position of the players as long as the music
is playing and their position after the music has stopped. In
the real world the music rarely stops (change is always taking
place) ; and if Ricardo intended the theory only in the second
sense, it clearly had only a limited application to the problems
of an ever-changing world. Nevertheless, it still held this
implication : that the sole hope of working-class improvement
lay in maintaining the pace of capital accumulation and
industrial progress and in limiting the rate of increase of the
wage-earning population. Later in the century, however,
economists (for instance Senior and J. S. Mill) were inclined
to stress the influence of changing custom to a greater extent
than Ricardo apparently did ; and in doing so abandoned

the inexorable rule of the " iron law " and substituted some
form of mixed supply and demand explanation in its
stead.

§ 5. Marx and the Power of Collective Bargaining.

Marx in particular stressed the influence of this factor of habit and custom ; and in the stress which he gave to this influence the theory in its practical implications assumed a new form. Marx followed Ricardo in thinking that the market price of labour-power could not for long depart from the value of the subsistence which the maintenance of that labour-power required, in so far as under capitalism labour-power was a commodity and its supply and its value were governed in a similar way to any other commodity. At the same time, labour-power had this difference from other commodities : it was attached to human beings ; and its supply was consequently governed in a unique sense by the " historical or social element ", which determined what human labourers required for a livelihood. " The value of labour," he said, " is formed by two elements—the one merely physical, the other historical or social. Its *ultimate limit* is determined by the *physical* element : that is to say, to maintain and produce itself, to perpetuate its physical existence, the working class must receive the necessaries absolutely indispensable for living and multiplying. . . . Besides this mere physical element, the value of labour is in every country determined by a *traditional standard of life*." It was this latter influence which explained the differences of wages between different countries, between different periods and even between different districts in the same country. Hence, when trade unions sought by combined action to advance the level of wages, they were not fighting a losing battle against an " iron law " which would assert itself in the long run : on the contrary, their action was itself part of the " social element ", and the gains which they won themselves helped to mould the "traditional standard of life" for the future. "The matter resolves itself into a question of the respective powers of the combatants." [1]

But while Marx stressed the influence of bargaining power, and his views have been classed under the *genus* of bargaining-theories or "force"-theories of wages, he did not depart so far from Ricardo as to treat the matter as entirely indeterminate and unpredictable. He did not suppose, for example, that it would be possible for trade union action indefinitely to raise wages and squeeze profits, so long as the capitalist wage-system existed. Much of the dominance of the classical law remained, even if its influence was powerfully refracted by the "social factor" of class conflict. Unlike Ricardo, however, Marx did not accept the Malthusian theory of population: in fact he explicitly repudiated it. Some other principle, accordingly, had to fill its place as determinant of the labour-supply. This principle was supplied by his theory of what he called "the industrial reserve army": a theory which he alternatively described as the law of "relative over-population". According to this, the supply of labour competing for jobs always tended to be kept in excess of the demand for it by a special feature of a capitalist wage-system: the special strength of the resistance that it put up in several ways to a rising level of wages.[2] These ways included the substitution of mechanical for human labour-power, the occurrence of periodic economic crises, which brought pressure to bear on the wage-level through the resulting unemployment, and the tendency to export capital abroad where cheaper reserves of labour could be tapped.

[1] *Value, Price and Profit*, ed. Eleanor Aveling, p. 85 *seq.*
[2] An important part of the reason for this was the tendency, under the existing economic system, for attention to be focused on the *rate* of return on capital (the rate of interest or the rate of profit), and the existence of rigidities in the system which resisted any tendencies that caused this rate to fall.

H

§ 6. The Wages-Fund Doctrine. Ricardo's qualification of
the subsistence-theory, by which he admitted that wages
might rise above the subsistence-level "for an indefinite
period in an improving society", encouraged a greater
emphasis to be placed on the aspect of demand. The doctrine
which provided this emphasis came to be known as the
Wages-fund doctrine ; and while it represented an important
shift of emphasis, it was regarded by its exponents as a
development of Ricardian notions rather than an alternative
to them. At this time it was common to treat capital as
consisting simply of " advances of wages " to workers—that
is, a sum devoted to paying wages to purchase labour-power
in advance of the completion and sale of the product. Hence,
it seemed natural to regard the demand for labour as being
furnished by the existing stock of capital : at least, as varying
directly with the accumulation of capital. The wage-level,
therefore, was to be found by a simple division sum : by
dividing the amount of capital (the wages-fund) that capitalists
were willing to lay out in the form of wage-advances by the
number of the wage-earning population seeking employment.
As John Stuart Mill put it : " Wages not only depend upon
the relative amount of capital and population, but cannot,
under the rule of competition, be affected by anything else."

The doctrine represented, therefore, a partial retreat from
the rigidity of the older view. It may, perhaps, be said to
have abandoned the attempt to provide a deterministic long-
term or " static " theory, and instead to have tried to explain
the movement of wages in a changing world. There was no
longer a single equilibrium-level to which wages must inevitably return, defined by the cost of production of labour-
power : there was a changing " natural-rate " defined by the
changing ratio of capital to population. True, the exponents
of this theory retained belief in the Malthusian law of population ; but generally (though not invariably) they were less

dogmatic about its over-riding influence on wages. *If* only the increase of population could be retarded and made to proceed at a slower pace than capital accumulation, the wage-level could rise. That this could happen they were not very confident,[1] but it was a possibility that they were no longer willing to deny.

Nevertheless, the theory was rigid enough in its own stern way. It was principally used to demonstrate the unbending corollary that bargaining power or trade union action was impotent to alter the wage-level as a whole, and that any measures which hindered the accumulation of capital (e.g. taxation of the rich to subsidize the poor) were bound to lower wages by depleting the wages-fund. The only hope of improvement for the workers lay in limiting the size of their own families and helping to increase the prosperity of their masters. For the better part of the Victorian age, this was the advice which was preached by economists to the working class and trade union leaders to show them the untutored folly of their methods. If one group of workers by legislation or trade union action secured an advance in wages, this must leave less of the wages-fund available for other workers, and so cause these others to have lower wages or to be unemployed. Conversely, if a group of workers were forced to accept an abnormally low wage, this did not really rob the working class as a whole : it merely left more of the wages-fund available to employ other groups of workpeople. Action, indeed, by trade unions or the State was more likely to have an adverse effect if it hindered the accumulation of capital or encouraged the labourers to breed faster than before. Mrs. Marcet, in her famous popular manual, made " Mrs. B." explain the matter to her pupil " Caroline " in this way :

[1] E.g. J. S. Mill, in his *Principles*, where he expresses a doubt whether the repeal of the Corn Laws was really calculated to yield any benefit to the working class (7th ed., Vol. I, 425).

"(the rate of wages) depends upon the proportion which capital bears to the labouring part of the population of the country. . . . It is this alone which regulates the rate of wages when they are left to pursue their natural course. It is this alone which creates or destroys the demand for labour. . . . When the number of labourers remains the same, the rate of wages will increase with the increase of capital and lower with the diminution of it : and if the amount of capital remain the same, the rate of wages will fall as the number of labourers increase, and rise as the number of labourers diminish ; or as mathematicians would express it, the rate of wages varies directly as the quantity of capital and inversely as the number of labourers. . . . Where there is capital the poor will always find employment, (and) the demand for labour is therefore proportioned to the extent of capital." [1] It followed that if the rich were taxed or their prosperity was otherwise impaired, so much less capital would be available to give employment. " The greatest evil that results from this provision for the poor (through Poor Law Relief) is that it lowers the price of labour ; the sum which the capitalist is obliged to pay as poor rates necessarily reduces the wages of his labourers, for if the tax did not exist, his capital being so much more considerable, the demand for labour and consequently its remuneration would be greater." [2] Charity or benevolence, whether public or private, could do nothing to alter this inexorable law of Political Economy.

In so far as changes in habit and custom were important in affecting what was regarded as a necessary standard and so in influencing the supply of labour, this remained as crucial a qualification of the Wages-Fund doctrine (at least, of the corollaries which it was used to support) as of the subsistence theory. If the influence of custom was important, then one

[1] *Conversations on Political Economy*, pp. 109, 117–18, 130.
[2] Ibid., p. 164.

way of changing the supply of labour, and so altering the
"natural price" of labour-power, was to raise wages; and
"interference" by trade unions to this end might beget the
very conditions which would make the rise permanent. As
long, however, as the Malthusian dogma held sway, people
were reluctant to believe that any extra bite of subsistence
could fail to encourage the birth and survival of an extra
mouth to eat it up, and so they attributed to custom little
more than a delaying influence on the natural laws governing
human increase. Not till late in the nineteenth century was
it realized that among persons of a higher standard of life
the birth-rate tends to be, not higher, but lower; [1] so that,
even allowing for the lower infant mortality which less
poverty entails, the rate of increase may be actually reduced
by a rise in the standard of life. A rise in wages may, therefore, have an important reaction on the supply of labour
in the opposite direction to that which the Malthusians
supposed.

The principle of the Economy of High Wages, to which
reference was made in the last chapter, supplied a second
important qualification to this doctrine; since it showed that
the productivity of labour was determined in a significant
degree by the level of wages; and if a rise in wages could
augment the efficiency of labour, it presumably would augment the employers' demand for that labour as well, stimulating them to lay out more funds in the purchase of labour.
Hence a rise of wages was capable of reacting, not only on the
supply conditions of labour, but also on the size of the
Wages-Fund itself, thereby shifting the demand for labour
in the opposite direction again from what the sponsors of
the Wages-Fund doctrine had assumed. Influenced by this
qualification and by altered notions as to the nature of capital,

---

[1] Nassau Senior was an exception to this statement. He, quite early,
gave this as a reason for expecting a steady rise in the level of wages.

economists towards the end of the century came to talk of the capital directed towards the employment of labour as constituting (in the words of Marshall) " not a fund but a flow ". Instead of a rigid fund which could only be augmented slowly with the growth of the surplus product of industry and of capital accumulated out of this surplus, circulating capital was thought of as a quickly varying quantity, which expanded or contracted according as the investing class found it more attractive to invest for a future profit than to spend for a present enjoyment. Income could quickly change its flow as between the two channels of spending and investment if the relative levels of the two outlets changed and exercised an altered attraction on the stream. At any given time it might be true that for a temporary period, perhaps a few months or a year, the *real* fund available out of which wages could be paid might be fixed, in the sense that the supply of food forthcoming was for the time being strictly limited in amount. For this reason it was often argued that even if larger sums of *money* were advanced to wage-earners, this would not increase the supply of necessaries forthcoming, and the result of the spending of the higher money wages would merely be for prices of necessaries to rise. But as Marx had pointed out in reply to an advocate of the Wages-Fund doctrine in 1865, this rigidity applies only to a short period. After a short interval the increased demand for necessaries would summon an increase in their supply, at the expense of the production of the luxuries that the rich had previously bought : " capital and labour would be transferred from the less remunerative to the more remunerative branches ; and this process of transfer would go on until the supply in the one department of industry had risen proportionately to the increased demand and had sunk in the other departments according to the decreased demand ".

§ 7. **The Theory of Marginal Productivity.** Realization that these qualifications were important led economists (for the most part) towards the end of the nineteenth century to abandon the Wages-Fund doctrine and to fasten attention on a demand-theory of a less rigid type. For some economists, most notably for Marshall, this newer view represented a significant shift of emphasis in the direction of treating the demand for labour as deriving from the product of labour rather than from any predetermined decisions made by capitalists as to the amount that they would invest. In treating circulating capital no longer as a fixed fund, but instead as a variable flow, it emphasized that any increase in the productivity of labour (whether due to a change in the efficiency of labour itself or of some other factor) would prompt a quickened flow of capital and so raise the demand for labour. But it would be unwise, I think, to over-emphasize the break with tradition that this newer view represented; and in the hands of many economists the theory of marginal productivity retained more of the essentials of the older doctrine than those who have emphasized its novel features often seem to have realized. The demand for labour, it is true, was treated, no longer as consisting in a fixed fund, but as being variable and quickly influenced by changes in labour-productivity; and the connection between this demand and changes in productivity was more precisely defined. But while allowance was made for the truths of the " economy of high wages ", many of the corollaries of the older doctrine were reinforced rather than weakened : for example, it was implied that, if the demand for labour was elastic, interference to raise wages above their " natural level " (unless it was coupled with increased productivity) would have the more damaging result of causing an actual shrinkage in the funds devoted to the employment of labour, instead of merely leaving this fund unchanged.

What chiefly contributed to the form which this new doctrine took was the increasing habit among economists in the final quarter of last century of thinking in terms of little bits of things (or increments) added or subtracted at the margin. Economists were at this time trying to explain the price of a commodity in terms of the extra utility, or satisfaction to consumers, yielded by the final or marginal unit of a given supply : given a supply of x hundred bushels of wheat, the price per bushel would measure the utility of the x-hundredth bushel to some one or other of the purchasers. It seemed to follow that the price of human labour-power could be explained in a similar way by its marginal utility to some purchaser of it. But labour did not satisfy consumers' wants directly, unless it was employed in domestic service : it only did so indirectly by turning out a product. Hence, given a certain supply of labour, its price was treated as being determined by the extra product that was yielded by the additional labour of the marginal unit of that supply. To the employer the worth of the labour-power he purchased consisted simply of the product it yielded him. In deciding what it would be worth while for him to pay to take on, say, an additional ten men, he would calculate how much would be added to the total output of his factory if he employed the additional ten. This " net product " (after allowing for any incidental expenses, such as extra raw materials involved in employing them) represented their worth to him and governed his *demand-price* for them—the amount he was willing to lay out in extra wages : the extent to which it was to his advantage to extend his " flow " of circulating capital. It followed that, given a certain supply of labour seeking employment, the competition of employers in bidding against one another for labour would tend to make the wage equal to this " net product " that the employment of the marginal units of the supply added to total output. Above this level wages could not go without causing the marginal units of the supply to be left unemployed, since these units would " cost " more than they were " worth ". Working with a fixed amount of plant and equipment, the extra product yielded by taking on more labour would generally be smaller the larger the staff of labour that was already employed : in other words, the attempt to extract more output from a given plant by employing additional labour was subject (beyond a point) to " diminishing returns ". Hence, there was always a definite limit to the amount of labour that it would be worth while for a firm, an industry and a whole country to employ at a given wage with a given amount of capital and natural resources. Given the supply of capital (or, to take it a stage further back, the rates of return on their capital which investors were demanding), given the supply of natural resources, and given the state of technique and the productivity of labour : then the level of wages at which everyone could get employment was rigidly determined. If labour demanded a higher price than this, unemployment must be the result.

This was, evidently, a much subtler doctrine than any of its predecessors, and more elegantly finished ; and many economists proceeded to hail it as a discovery that furnished a complete and final theory, not only of wages, but of the distribution of income in general. Professor J. B. Clark, one of its original exponents, even declared it to be a " natural law " of wages which held true independently of time and of place ; and Jevons, with hint of a profound meaning in the words, spoke ambiguously of the worker receiving " the due value of his produce ". It certainly seemed final and satisfying to many to be able to say that labour's reward varied with labour's " productivity " ; from which it was too often implied or presumed that wages measured what the services performed by labour were " worth " to society in some sense more fundamental than that this was the price which the market placed upon labour in a given (and possibly alterable) set of circumstances. But " productivity ", " service ", " worth " are ambiguous terms ; and wiser opinion was aware that the theory did not by itself constitute a complete theory of wages. A reason for its incompleteness (which it shares with other demand-theories) was that it included nothing to tell one how the supply of labour was determined : this it had to assume to be a given quantity in order to find what was the marginal net product of labour. It also left many things unsaid about how the supply of capital was determined. While the theory defined more precisely the way in which wages were related to productivity, it added little to our knowledge of the complex of interacting factors on which this productivity depended. As Marshall said : " This doctrine has sometimes been put forward as a theory of wages. But there is no valid ground for any such pretension. The doctrine that the earnings of a worker tend to be equal to the net product of his work has by itself no real meaning ; since in order to estimate net product, we have to take for granted all the expenses of production of the commodity on which he works, other than his wages." [1]

It is important always to bear in mind that the " marginal net product " of labour depends, not only on the supply of labour, but also on the supply of all the other factors of production ; and when this has been said, the theory is robbed of much of its apparent simplicity and finality. If labour is the relatively scarce factor, and the others plentiful, the marginal net product of labour will be high ; and competition for labour will enable it to command a high price. For example, in a new country, rich in undeveloped resources,

[1] *Principles of Economics*, 518. Marshall, however, adds that this objection is " not valid against a claim that the doctrine throws into clear light the action of one of the causes that govern wages ". In his first edition he spoke of it as containing " a part, but only a small part, of the Law of Wages ".

but still thinly populated, new settlers can produce considerable wealth by the labour of their hands ; but when natural resources have been more fully developed and the region has become populous, it will generally be much less easy for new settlers unaided by capital to wring a living from the soil, and labour consequently will tend to be cheap. Again, if capital exacts a high rate of interest and is scarce, this will be a factor tending to depress the marginal net product of labour and the level of wages, particularly if the number of persons willing to work for a pittance is plentiful. Moreover, the efficiency with which industry is organized will also affect the productivity of labour ; as will the existing state of technique, which will determine how dispensable or indispensable human labour-power is—how easily mechanical power can be substituted for it—and the distribution of consumers' demand between different products—between goods which require much labour to produce them and goods which require little. The marginal net product of labour will depend upon all these things as well as upon the intrinsic efficiency of labour itself ; almost any change, indeed, in the price of anything else is likely to affect it.

§ 8. **Marshall and Supply and Demand.** Marshall, who was more alive than many economists to the complexity of the economic world, where all things are subject to " mutual interaction ", attempted to provide a synthetic view, in which the forces which affected the supply of labour and the forces which affected the demand for labour were combined. On the whole, the theory which he reached was less rigidly deterministic than the traditional doctrines : for example, it allowed some scope to the influence of collective bargaining by trade unions on wages, through its effect not only on the efficiency, but also on the " supply-price " of labour.

We have seen that the employers' demand for labour is

dependent on a number of things. A principal thing on which it will be dependent will be the supply of capital—on how plentiful and cheap it is for the existing or prospective business man to raise. Marshall regarded this supply as being determined over a period of time by the ability and willingness of investors to divert their income from immediate consumption and to save and invest it instead. At any one instant of time, it is true, the capital available is a fixed amount dependent on the actions of investors in the past ; but it is a stock which in the course of time can be added to or reduced by investors in adding new savings to it or in diverting part of the stock to swell their current expenditure. But while this stock of capital is elastic over a period of time, it remains elastic only within certain limits. These limits are set by the preference which investors have for spending money at once rather than putting it by to bring in an income in the future. Most people, except misers, it is said (though some have disputed it), prefer to have £100 to spend now than the promise of £101 in a year's time, perhaps than the promise of £105 or £106 in a year's time, even if this promise is absolutely trustworthy and certain to be kept. This preference for present joys has been termed their " time-preference " or their " discount of the future " ; and represents what Marshall considered to be the sacrifice involved in " waiting " or saving. This " cost " involved in saving will act as a brake on the flow of capital into industry, and, when expressed in terms of the sum of money necessary to overcome this reluctance on the part of investors, will constitute the " supply-price " of capital. This " supply-price " necessary to overcome the resistance to saving or waiting, and to attract capital into industry, will generally be greater for a large than for a small annual supply of savings : indeed, it may be very low for a small amount of new capital, since the rich might save part of their income which they could not find ways of spending, even if they were to receive little or no return on it when invested. The supply-prices of different quantities of new capital (of differently sized additions to the stock) can, therefore, be expressed in what Marshall called a " schedule of supply-prices ", or a supply-curve—a curve linking up the different supply-prices of different amounts.[1] If one wished to contrast this view with the Wages-Fund doctrine, one could say that a supply-schedule of this type defined the limits within which the Wages-Fund might vary in the course of time ; but that it treated this fund as being elastic, expanding year by year under the influence of a bright prospect of profit by drawing to itself a larger proportion of the investors' incomes, and contracting if the prospect of profit was sufficiently poor.

With regard to the supply of labour, Marshall apparently considered that analogous conditions applied. While he was cautious in his statements concerning the supply of labour *in general*, as distinct from the supply of labour of a particular type, it seems clear that he regarded this as being elastic in some measure—as changing in response to changes in the wage-level—even though this elasticity was very much smaller than the older economists had imagined. The wage-level would, then, tend to be determined by the two sets of forces which defined the conditions of demand for labour and the conditions of its supply ; and under competition wages would have a long-run tendency to be at that level where the marginal net product of the available labour-supply was equal to its marginal supply-price. Yet " wages are not governed by demand-price, nor by supply-prices, but by the whole set of causes which govern demand and supply ".[2]

---

[1] It is to be noted that these, properly defined, are supply-prices of given *rates* of investment. There may also be maintenance-prices of different *stocks* of capital ; but the relevant maintenance-price will generally be much lower than the prevailing return on capital, and to this extent inoperative.

[2] Marshall, *Principles* (8th ed.), p. 532.

§ 9. The Supply of Labour. Whether the supply of labour to industry in general (as distinct from one particular trade or locality) varies directly with changes in the wage-level has been the subject of considerable discussion. The phrase "the supply of labour" can, of course, be used in a number of senses. First, it may be applied to the *number of workers* seeking employment. This will vary, not only with the total population, but with the proportion of the population which is proletarianized or without an alternative livelihood, and so is driven by circumstances into the labour market to seek employment for wages. Secondly, it may include the *number of hours* which each worker is willing to work, so that a unit of labour is treated as consisting of a "man-hour" of work, and the supply of labour as being increased by any increase in the length of the working day or the working week. Thirdly, it may be stretched to include the *intensity of work*, so that a unit of labour becomes some unit expressing the energy-output of work, and the supply of labour is regarded as being increased when workers work harder than before. On the other hand, changes in the *skill* with which work is applied, as distinct from changes in the intensity of work (in so far as a line can be drawn between them), seem better treated as affecting the quality of labour rather than its amount.

At first sight it would appear that the higher are wages, the greater will be the ability and the inducement to work, and hence the greater the supply of labour must be ; and *vice versa*. But there is a crucial consideration which operates in the other direction ; namely, that the reason (as was seen in Chapter I) for so large a section of the population coming into the labour market and hiring themselves for wages lies in their poverty—in their absence of an alternative livelihood. The poorer is the wage-earning class, and the smaller any reserve that workers have to fall back upon, the cheaper the price at which they are willing to sell their labour-power ;

and *vice versa*. The lower the income which people have, the higher the valuation they put on each additional shilling; or the more they are willing to do in order to obtain an extra shilling: in other words, the lower is the supply-price of their labour in terms of money or of anything else.[1] The influence of this factor may well be powerful enough to make the relation between the wage-level and the supply of labour, as was seen in the last chapter (see p. 54), the opposite of what at first sight might be supposed. A fall in wages may mean an increase in the supply of labour in three ways: it may force a larger number of women and young workers to seek employment under pressure of poverty, and it may bring pressure on existing wage-earners to work longer hours or to increase the intensity of work. This process will, of course, have its limit: for example, if the length and intensity of work are pushed beyond a certain point, it may exert such an influence on health and in shortening the working-life of the average worker as to react thereby in a reduction of the labour-supply in the course of time. Conversely, a rise in wages may encourage workers to take out part of the benefit in increased leisure or more leisurely methods of work rather than in increased earnings. As we have seen there is also evidence that a change in the wage-level may react in a similar way on the total population, through its influence on the birth-rate, at least where knowledge of birth-control methods is widely diffused.

[1] This is to say that the " marginal utility of income " will be high or low according to the size of the income received. It is a matter of convenience, rather than of principle, whether this is expressed in the form of a single supply-curve which slopes *back*, or in a series of movements of the whole supply-curve to new positions as the marginal utility of income changes. For purposes of statistical study of concrete data the former is the more serviceable; but for purposes of analysing the separate causes of change, the latter is the more convenient, and the distinction implied by it between the two kinds of movement of supply is important.

§ **10. Inventions and Wages.** An important influence on the demand for labour of which little has hitherto been said is the state of industrial technique. If this were unalterable and of a kind which required that machinery should always be staffed by a fixed number of workers (e.g. two men to each engine, a minder and two piecers to so many spinning-mules), then it would be the case, as the disciples of the Wage-Fund doctrine seem to have assumed, that changes in the demand for labour were entirely dependent on changes in the amount of capital : more capital would mean more machines *and* equivalently more men to work them.[1] But complete rigidity of technical conditions, while it may be the case at any one moment of time, clearly does not hold over a period of time long enough for the type of machine and the mode of its operation to be altered : larger lathes or larger locomotives can be introduced and still be operated by the same number of persons as before, or automatic looms can be introduced, more of which are operated by one weaver than before.

In industry in general the capital invested will divide along two main streams. One will go as fixed capital to set up plant and machinery, the other as circulating capital into the purchase of raw materials and labour-power. This second stream again divides into two further ones—the one spent on materials, and the other (variable capital, as Marx called it, or a revolving Wages-Fund) on hiring labour. The capital will tend to be distributed along these streams so that the " level " of profit at the end of each stream is approximately equal—so that the last £ spent in wages adds as much to the net product of the business as the last £ spent on machinery. At any one time this will apply both to a particular business

---

[1] Even so, unless the ratio of capital to labour were the same in all industries, shifts in demand between products embodying relatively much and relatively little labour, compared to capital, would exert an influence on the demand for labour apart from any change in the supply of capital.

and to all businesses taken together, including those firms which are making machines for use in other industries.

The proportions in which it is most profitable to distribute the capital along these streams will differ in different industries according to the technical character of their productive processes. But in industry as a whole in any given state of machine-technique a certain proportion will exist which is the most profitable; and any flow of new capital will tend to distribute itself in these proportions. It will be fairly clear that, if an invention is introduced which enables machines to be produced more cheaply or increases their efficiency, the effect will be to make investment in machinery more profitable than it was before, and so to encourage a *larger* proportion of the funds invested to go into machinery and a *smaller* proportion to be used as a wages-fund to employ labour on operating these machines. It was this reason which Marx adduced to show that the demand for labour did not increase proportionately with the accumulation of capital, but that as capital accumulated the demand for labour tended to fall relatively: " it will still increase, but increase in a constantly diminishing ratio as compared with the increase of capital ".

It has traditionally been supposed that this kind of substitution (of capital invested and locked up in machinery and other forms of fixed capital for capital devoted at any one time to purchase of labour) will also be the result of a rise of wages. The reason given for this view has been that a rise in the cost of labour will reduce the profitability of capital invested in the employment of labour as compared with the profitability of capital invested in machinery, thereby encouraging more capital to flow along the latter stream and less along the former.

But an objection to this line of reasoning at once springs to the mind. Is not machinery also the product of labour—

I

" stored-up labour " or " dead labour ", as Marx called it, by contrast with " living labour " ? And if this be true, will not a rise in wages have a similar effect on the cost of machinery as on the cost of the labour it displaces, so that no shift need occur in the relative attractiveness of the two streams along which capital flows ? This objection, however, ignores the fact that a given percentage rise of wages will reduce profits proportionately more where wages are a large part of the total value produced (and profits an equivalently small part) than in the converse case where wages are a small part (and profits an equivalently large part). Since more of the value produced is apt to go to profits when much capital is used than when little is used, any rise of wages is likely to exert a bias in favour of technical methods that are relatively capital-using. It is possible that this effect may be offset by a rise in the rate of interest occasioned by the rise of wages.[1] But unless employers borrow all their capital in the capital market, this offset is unlikely to be more than a partial one ; and Professor D. H. Robertson seems to be justified in claiming that it " would not, in any ordinary case, destroy the reasons for supposing that [a rise of wages] would stimulate the substitution of capital for labour ".[2]

The type of invention of which we have been speaking is generally termed " labour saving ". Not all technical change is of this kind. The influence of some is " capital saving ", and the results will be the converse of what we have said above, so far as effects on the demand for labour and the demand for capital are concerned. Experience suggests, however, that the influence of invention has been *preponder-*

---

[1] According to modern interest-theory a rise of wages may have the effect of raising the rate of interest by increasing the " transactions demand " for money.

[2] Sir Dennis Robertson, *Lectures on Economic Principles*, Volume II, p. 113. The above paragraph is an emendation of what appeared in previous editions : an emendation in deference to Professor Robertson's criticism.

antly in a " labour saving " direction. This sort of technical change will tend to reduce wages *relatively*,[1] i.e. reduce labour's proportionate share of the total product. The question which has been one of considerable dispute, however, is whether it will reduce wages *absolutely*, in the sense of reducing the real earnings of workers in general. If technical change of this kind has the result of reducing the amount of labour required to produce a certain output, it would seem that this must have the effect of reducing either the amount of employment available or the rate of wages at which employment can be secured. Economists in the past have usually maintained, however, that there will be two sorts of compensating effect of technical change, which will mean that the total real earnings of labour will rise in the long run, even when the *initial* effect of the invention is an apparent shrinkage in demand for labour. First of these compensations is the cheapening of goods as a result of the new technique, which may increase the purchasing-power of a given money-wage, and so may offset or more than offset.(so far as total working-class earnings are concerned) any tendency for money-wage-rates to decline. Second of these compensations is the expansion of output which it is claimed will follow as a result of the cheapening of the cost of producing this output now that improved technical methods are in use. If demand is sufficiently elastic, output is likely to expand in the long-period so as to make the number of jobs available as large (or larger) after the introduction of the new technique as before.

Regarding the first of these forms of compensation, it may be said that it is necessary (if the initial decline in demand for labour is to be offset), not merely that wage-earners should

---

[1] Although it will be without any such effect under the special assumptions (constant short-period costs) employed recently by Dr. Kalecki in his analysis of the effects of monopoly on the share of labour (*Essays in the Theory of Economic Fluctuations*, p. 24).

gain *something* in cheaper goods resulting from the invention, but that these cheapened goods should compose an important part of wage-earners' consumption. If we remember that some two-thirds of working-class expenditure in the past has been on the products of the building trades and of agriculture, this compensating effect of mechanical invention on real wages may be considerably smaller than has often been supposed. Perhaps the technical improvements which have most benefited wage-earners *qua* consumers are the steamship and the extension of railways in agricultural countries overseas, since these contributed to that cheapening of foodstuffs in the latter part of the nineteenth century from which the increase of real wages in that period so largely derived. However, *some* compensating effect of this sort is likely to occur.

As regards the second type of compensation, some economists in recent years have been inclined to question the optimism with which it used to be assumed that in nearly all cases this would occur on a large enough scale to offset the original displacement of labour by a labour-saving machine. It has been pointed out that the elasticity of demand for goods in general (as distinct from individual commodities) cannot be very large as long as the total income of the mass of the population is constant ; and demand (and hence output) is only likely to increase if their incomes first increase. How, it may be asked, can the compensation of increased sales and output get seriously under way, if the initial effect of the invention in technique is to reduce employment ? The answer to this objection which is usually given is that an important (and immediate) effect of technical change is to stimulate *investment*. Since labour-saving inventions tend to " put more power behind the human elbow ", their first effect is to cause a demand for more machines in order to raise the ratio of mechanical equipment to labour. If this means more employment in the machine-making trades, and hence an addition to the incomes of those connected with these trades, demand for other goods may increase as well. Hence, as long as technical change is occurring, this process of building up the stock of capital equipment to a higher level will tend to have a buoyant influence upon employment and incomes. But it has to be remembered that this compensating effect of stimulated investment only operates as long as this building-up process is going on. In this sense it is a " once-for-all " effect, and not necessarily a permanent effect. Once it is over, the fact remains that less labour is required to produce a given quantity of output than before ; and unless some permanent influences tending to raise either investment or people's expenditure on consumption have come into the picture, the ultimate result may still tend to be a fall in the level of employment.[1]

[1] Cf. for a full development of this argument, Joan Robinson, *Essays in the Theory of Employment*, pp. 132–36.

CHAPTER V

WAGES AND BARGAINING-POWER

§ 1. The " Laissez-faire " View. Underlying the differences
of form in which the theories of wages described in the last
chapter were stated, there was, as we have seen, a more fundamental question : is the wage-level dependent, wholly or in
part, upon the bargaining powers of employers and employed,
or is it determined ultimately by economic forces to which
the strength of the two contracting parties is irrelevant and
which bargaining-power alone cannot bend ? Bargaining-
power is, of course, a vague word which can be used with
different meanings, and may cover a variety of factors, from
monopolistic action in concert to the possession of information
regarding market conditions, or the security of some reserve
in the background to stiffen an individual in the bargaining
process. There are few, if any, who would deny all influence
to bargaining-power in any of these senses, just as there are
few, if any, who would endow it with limitless power : the
difference is one of emphasis, and the varieties of emphasis
are great. In the main, however, one can say that writers on
the wages-question have been grouped in two camps round
this direct and practical question : is the *permanent* influence
which either a trade union can exert through collective-bar-
gaining and strike-action, or the State can exert by establishing
a legal minimum wage, so small as to be negligible (unless it
be an influence in a harmful direction by hampering production), or is it sufficiently important for any theory of wages
which neglects it to be a deceptive guide to practical affairs ?

The former of these two views—that the permanent influence of such action is negligible—which we may call the

118

laissez-faire theory of wages, was generally held by economists in the middle of last century, when the growing strength of trade unions was arousing attention and alarm.   John Stuart Mill, for example, argued that for the State to fix a minimum wage would be useless, unless at the same time it took action to control the number of births (a view which he later modified).   Jevons devoted a large part of his inaugural lecture at Owens College, Manchester, to an attack on trade unions, and in a popular primer declared that " there is no reason whatever to think that trades unions have had any permanent effect in raising wages in the majority of trades ".[1]   Even Lord Brassey, who was so keen to show that cheap labour " seems to exercise the same enervating influence (on employers) as the delights of Capua on the soldiers of Hannibal ", preached that trade unions were better employed in spreading information among their members than in trying to enforce higher wages.   But even while the sternness of Victorian doctrine has been relaxed, this view, in its substantial emphasis, still has powerful exponents to-day, as the following examples will show.   Professor Robbins once wrote : " The idea that Trade Unions can, in the majority of cases, permanently raise the wages of their members dies very hard. . . .   In the majority of cases, at least, this belief is doomed to disappointment.   In the long run it is very unlikely that Trade Unions can permanently raise wages above the competitive level."   And again : " The sole result of the establishment on a large scale of minimum wages above the competitive level would be to cause unemployment and diminish production." [2]   Sir Hubert Henderson expressed a similar view.   " The wage-level in the long run," he asserted, " is airly rigidly determined. . . .   It is . . . an illusion to suppose that the general level of

[1] *A Primer of Political Economy*, p. 64 ; and his *Importance of Diffusing a Knowledge of Political Economy* (1866).
[2] Lionel Robbins, *Wages*, pp. 67–68 and 72–73.

wages can be appreciably and permanently raised by Trade Union action, except in so far as it increases the efficiency of the workers or incidentally stimulates the efficiency of the employers." [1]

§ 2. The " Normal " Competitive Wage. The first reason on which this view relies is the effect of competition in keeping the price of labour at the highest level which industry can afford to pay. " It is a mistake to suppose," said J. S. Mill, " that competition merely keeps down wages. It is equally the means by which they are kept up." " No capitalists can for more than a year or two make unusual profits," said Jevons, " because if they do, other capitalists are sure to hear of it and try to do likewise. The result will be that the demand for labourers in that kind of trade will increase." Mr. J. R. Hicks has suggested that the desire of each employer to secure high-quality labour will be a special influence inducing him to over-bid other employers for labour, in the hope that the reputation of being a high-wage employer will attract to him the best workers in the trade.

But supposing that wages are pushed, by trade union or State action, above this competitive level, what will prevent them from staying there ? Employers will get smaller profits, and more of the product of industry will go as wages to its workers ; but what is the matter with that ? Here a second argument comes into play : the argument that what will prevent this is the elasticity in the demand for labour. To avoid misunderstanding one must add that it is not denied that wages *might* be kept permanently at this higher level if enough force were used. What is maintained is that this cannot occur without causing such a large shrinkage in the demand for labour in the long run as to cause greater damage to the earnings of labour through unemployment than was

[1] *Supply and Demand*, p. 145.

gained in the higher wage, and to give rise to pressure (in the shape of the unemployed army competing for employment) to reduce wages again—for example, to reduce them, if not in the "protected" trades, in the unorganized trades and in occupations unprotected by a minimum-wage.

It is not nowadays generally denied that action to raise wages might be successful where it led to a proportional increase of efficiency; although it is sometimes implied that if this were the case, employers would have found it in their interest to raise wages previously.[1] Nor is it denied that there are particular trades where the demand for labour is fairly inelastic (e.g. where the demand for the product is inelastic, where labour cannot be substituted by machinery, and where the supply of other factors of production is very inelastic so that there is a large element of squeezable surplus or rent). In these cases the earnings of the workers could be increased, without any equivalent reduction in real wages elsewhere. What is denied is that this state of affairs can exist in all industries, or even in the majority of industries : that for labour *in general* the demand can be inelastic. The reasons for which the demand for labour in general is thought to have a fairly high degree of elasticity (that is, to contract or expand considerably for any given change in the price of labour-power) are two. First, it is held that the supply of capital is itself elastic, in the sense that if the return that the capitalists get is reduced, as it will tend to be by any rise in wage-cost, the amount of new capital which capitalists will accumulate and invest over the future will shrink. This shrinkage is likely to occur, both because capitalists have smaller incomes out of

---

[1] The case stressed by Mr. Rowe in his *Wages in Practice and Theory*, where the rise in wages increases, not the efficiency of the worker, but the efficiency of the employers' organization, seems to have a more doubtful relevance to the competence of such action to raise wages without causing unemployment, since the bias that will be given to industrial reorganization by a rise in wages-cost may be a labour-saving one.

which to invest, and because they will tend to invest a smaller proportion of this income. The second reason consists in what has been called the Principle of Variation : the fact that (as was seen at the end of the last chapter) capital itself may change its form, a larger proportion of it going as fixed capital into plant and equipment—into putting " more power behind the elbow ", as Americans term it—and a smaller proportion as a Wages-Fund to hire human labour-power. This may occur in two ways, both of which may be the consequence of a rise in the wages-cost of output : it may occur in the form of a change of technical methods which substitutes machines for labour in each industry, or in the form of a shift in the relative importance of different industries in the direction of a relative decline of those lines of production which use a high proportion of labour to fixed capital, and an expansion of those which are more highly mechanized and less " labour-using ". Both of these changes will have the effect of contracting the field of employment for labour, thereby bringing pressure to bear to reduce the wage-level to " normal " again.

In any given short-period of time neither of these types of change will, of course, occur. Both the amount of capital and the forms in which it is invested will be fairly rigidly fixed ; and the demand for labour will be correspondingly inelastic. This the *laissez-faire* view does not deny. Even so, it is maintained that a rise in wages which is not accompanied by a corresponding rise in efficiency is likely to cause *some* shrinkage of employment, since to employ the same labour-force at a higher wage-level would require an actual increase in the total wages-bill of the country, which is unlikely to be forthcoming, save where technical conditions are absolutely rigid (e.g. to sack a man would mean laying an engine idle as well), or in exceptional boom conditions, when employers are eager to fulfil outstanding contracts, credit-conditions are easy and unusual business optimism prevails. But

over a longer period of time, when opportunity has been given
for technical changes to occur as well as for the total stock of
capital to be affected by changes in the annual flow of new
investments, the demand for labour (it is argued) will be
considerably reduced as compared with what it would have
been if wages had remained at their normal competitive level,
as fixed by conditions of supply and demand.

§ 3. Two Qualifications. In recent years a good deal of
criticism has been levelled by economists against at least the
more rigid forms of this *laissez-faire* view ; and a considerable
literature of controversy on the subject has accumulated.
Even in the nineteenth century, of course, trade unionists
and their champions [1] opposed the current versions of this
doctrine and from time to time some economist emphasized
some important qualification of it.   But to-day disagreement
with the doctrine is more general ; and a number of new
arguments, as well as older arguments refurbished, have been
advanced in support of a sceptical view.

Before we refer to some of these arguments, there are two
observations to be made, which, though they are hardly in
dispute, are not infrequently overlooked.   In the first place,
even if the *laissez-faire* view, as we have outlined it, were
true in its most rigid form, it would not follow that the
" normal " level of wages which it defined was " natural "
in the sense that it was imposed by the natural order of things
and must hold true whatever the form of society and the
prevailing social institutions might be.   Nor would it follow
that this wage-level represented the unique " productivity "
of labour, or its " contribution " to society, in any sense more
profound than that this was the valuation which a competitive market placed upon it in a given set of circumstances,

[1] Most notably, of course, Mr. and Mrs. Webb in their *Industrial
Democracy*.

and that this was the price that the relative plentifulness or scarcity of labour-power (compared with the other requisites of production, the general organization of industry and the general conditions of demand) enabled it to obtain. Even if it were true that unemployment would invariably follow if wages were pushed above this level, *other things remaining the same*, it would be as true to say that the high level of interest or profits which capitalists were demanding was a " cause " of this unemployment as to say that it was the unique result of the level of wages.

Secondly, as was seen in Chapter III, it does not follow that everything which reduces the aggregate earnings of labour is contrary to the welfare of labour ; and it does not follow, as, for example, Jevons confidently assumed, that " we cannot possibly increase the welfare of the people by lessening labour, the source of wealth ".[1] In certain circumstances interference to raise wages above their competitive level, even though it may contract the total field of employment, may nevertheless promote the welfare of the working class in general. This is most evidently the case where a rise in wages, for example in overtime rates, leads to a shortening of the hours of labour : even if their earnings are reduced thereby, workers may gain more in improved health and greater leisure than they lose in earnings. Similarly, in the case of the so-called " sweated trades ", to which reference will be made in the next chapter : there is a gain from the removal of women and children from the wretched exploitation of low-paid work under abominable conditions which will probably far outweigh in the long run any loss of earnings resulting from the elimination of such employments. The practical importance of this qualification has often been belittled on the ground that curtailed employment in such cases is more likely to take the form of complete destitution for some than diminished earnings coupled with

[1] *The State in Relation to Labour* (1894 ed.), p. 74.

more leisure all round ; and the damage to welfare resulting from the former will be particularly great, and probably too great to be worth while.   But for a number of reasons which are touched on below, this does not seem necessarily to be the case.

This consideration, however, leads directly to a more general one : that so far as concerns one set of forces on which the normal competitive wage depends, namely, the supply-conditions of labour, these, as we have seen, will be in large part dependent on the prevailing standard of life of the workers ; with the result that the so-called " normal " wage turns out to be in fact a position of neutral (or even unstable) equilibrium which can be shifted, a fall in wages producing the very change in conditions (a lowered supply-price of labour) calculated to perpetuate that lower level ; and conversely with a rise in wages.   Hence the amount of work extracted from the labourer in proportion to what he receives is capable of being influenced by such a factor as bargaining strength over a considerable range ; and even though an increase in the bargaining strength of labour might not be able to increase the total earnings of labour, there is a range within which it could appreciably modify to its own advantage the terms of its exchange of effort against earnings.   This is apparently what Marshall had in mind when he stressed the fact that, if workers bargained individually and unsupported by the collective bargaining of a trade union, they were generally in an inferior bargaining position, and that this inferiority caused them to sell their labour-power at an abnormally cheap price.   The lowness of the standard of life may then be the principal reason for the supply-conditions of labour being such as to keep the wage-level low—" poverty breeds poverty ", as has been popularly said.   It will follow that all similar factors which affect the social and economic conditions of the wage-earning class will likewise affect the terms of the wage-contract : for example, institutional changes such as the elimination of the independent peasantry or artisanry, which will not only increase directly the *number* of persons competing in the labour market, but by removing from all wage-earners the option of an alternative livelihood will make them more economically dependent than before. Such factors, indeed, will exert a fundamental influence on the wage-contract; since, as was seen in Chapter I, without the creation of a dependent proletariat, a capitalist wage-system would have lacked a crucial part of its historical basis.

§ 4. **Standards of Consumption and Investment.** One line of criticism of the traditional view has amounted to a claim that the demand for labour, even over a long period, is much less elastic than this view supposed, since the existing stock of capital and the rate of new investment are likely to be little affected by changes in wages. Perhaps it is rather misleading to speak here about the demand being " inelastic " (since much of this criticism has been concerned with moving situations and not with stationary conditions); and it is more simple and direct to say that there is much greater scope for wages to be raised, and for other incomes to be squeezed, without adversely affecting investment and employment, than was formerly assumed. Firstly, it may be the case that a large part of the effect of any rise in the wage-level will be taken up in squeezing rent-elements and various sorts of monopoly-gains in other incomes, without this squeezing exercising directly any deterrent effects on production and employment. Secondly, even though the investing class is thereby made poorer (which might seem likely to reduce their ability to invest), this may not lead to any appreciable shrinkage in their investments in new capital; since although their present income is reduced so is their future income likely to be also, with the result that they may be encouraged to invest a larger *proportion* of their income than before. In other words, the reduction in capitalists' income may reduce their spending but not their investment. This is rendered the more probable by the fact that the expenditure of the rich is so largely conventional, depending on customs and standards of consumption which are themselves products of a high income-level. It becomes specially probable when the national income is expanding, and the effect of rising wages may be to cause capitalists' income, and hence their acquisition of more lavish class-standards of expenditure, to grow more slowly than would otherwise have been the case.

At any rate, it is obviously fantastic to hold that economic theory can demonstrate (as has often been implied in the past, even if it has not been explicitly stated) that any attempt to raise wages in a sweated trade, and to eliminate the exploitation of wretchedly overworked and ill-paid workers, must necessarily reduce the fund of capital devoted to employing labour in the future, rather than reduce by that amount the pleasures of the rich.

It must, however, be added that there are obvious limits to this line of argument. Standards of expenditure once acquired are apt to be rigid ; and these may set an upward limit to any rise of wages that appreciably eats into the income of the capitalist class (as distinct from merely preventing it from rising in times of prosperity). Something like a " strike of capital " may be the reaction if the slice of the cake that goes to capital is suddenly or greatly cut down. This is, at any rate, a possibility that has to be reckoned with so long as control over production and investment is in private hands. A complicating factor is that to-day an increasingly large part of new investment in industry does not come from subscriptions by private individuals to new share-issues, but is undertaken directly by large companies out of reserves accumulated out of undistributed profits over a period of years. It is true that if the profits which accrue to such companies are reduced sufficiently, their ability to accumulate these reserves and to invest from them must be reduced. But it is not impossible that, if their total profits are narrowed, they may choose to maintain their investments at the expense of reducing that part of the total which they distribute as dividends to shareholders; and as far as the *inducement* to invest is concerned, it is not clear that the investment policy of large corporations is responsive in any very simple or direct manner to changes in the expected rate of profit. Probably more important in this connection are certain considerations to be mentioned in § 6, which suggest that changes in the level of money-wages of their own employees may not be a very important influence in determining the amount of profit that such companies are able to earn. It has also to be remembered that, not only direct investment by companies out of their reserves, but also investment by various kinds of public bodies is playing an increasingly important rôle to-day; and the latter type of investment is not controlled by the profit-motive. In a socialist system, where investment and production were completely controlled by the State, this particular limit of which we have spoken, set by rigid standards of expenditure of an investing class, would no longer, of course, exist.

§ 5. Imperfect Competition in the Labour Market. It has been mentioned above (in Chapter III, § 1) that, even when competition is perfect, it is not necessarily in the interest of employers to secure to their workers a wage adequate to their long-period health and efficiency, or to extend to them the advantage of economic security. But the criticism of the *laissez-faire* view about which most has recently been heard consists in a denial that perfect competition exists in the labour market, and hence a denial of the effectiveness of the force to which J. S. Mill referred as " the means by which wages are kept up ". Adam Smith originally pointed out, in a classic passage, that " masters are always and everywhere in a sort of tacit, but constant and uniform, combination not to raise the wages of labour above their actual rate. To violate this combination is everywhere a most unpopular action, and a sort of reproach to a master among his neighbours and equals ". This is probably even more true to-day with the growth of the large firm and of monopolistic combination on such an extensive scale. Where this is the case, the competitive bidding of one master against another, tending to force up the wage to the " normal " competitive level, will be absent ; and it will profit the employer (given some inelasticity in the supply of labour) to employ *less* labour than would otherwise be the case at a *lower* rate. In other words, the wage will be *below* the " marginal net product " of labour. Even where no such combination exists as that of which Adam Smith speaks, the immobility of labour, due to lack of information or the expense of moving to another job, may give each employer a sort of limited monopoly over his own private " pool " of labour, because this labour is sluggish in moving off to another employer, and the extra inducement which has to be offered to attract workers from another employment is sufficiently large to discourage employers from poaching on one another's preserves. Measures which tend to make an employee reluctant to leave his employment with a particular firm reinforce this influence : for example, chance of promotion after long service, or attachment to some co-partnership or pensions scheme connected with the firm. Reference has already been made to measures which are aimed at reducing " labour-turnover " in industry, or the speed with which men change their occupations. Undoubtedly a high labour-turnover imposes special costs of its own on industry. For example, one of the first

K

tractor-factories to be built in the U.S.S.R. about 1929 found for a time that, as other factories of similar type were built, it was rapidly becoming merely a training-school for new workers, who came in from the countryside to be taught the work and then moved on elsewhere, in hope of rapid promotion in a new and less-well-staffed enterprise, with the result that its costs were greatly inflated and its output-plans could not be fulfilled. But while these special costs exist, there is also another aspect of the matter ; and part of the attraction to employers of the various methods of reducing labour-turnover which have been so much canvassed, particularly in America, has undoubtedly lain in the relaxation of an upward competitive pressure on the wage-level which they yield. The fact that employers as a class are so evidently apprehensive as to the effects of any unusual competition among employers for labour seems to indicate how restricted such competition generally is. When Employment Exchanges, for example, were first introduced in this country in 1911, some employers expressed the fear that these might encourage too great a mobility of labour ; and when in war-time labour became scarce, restrictions were quickly introduced to prevent a worker from changing his employment and moving elsewhere under the attraction of a higher wage.[1]

§ 6. **The Influence of Monopoly and of Excess Capacity.** In recent economic writings two factors have been given prominence which have rather drastically altered the setting of discussion about wage problems. First of these is the prevalence

---

[1] During the First World War this took the form for a time of " leaving certificates ", which a worker in war-industry had to obtain before he could change his job. In the Second World War it took the form chiefly of the Essential Work Order, under which a worker could neither leave his job nor be dismissed without official permission ; but at the same time the worker was awarded certain guarantees, including the guarantee of a minimum wage.

of a large degree of monopoly (or, at least, of imperfect competition) not only in the labour market itself (of which we spoke in the last paragraph) but in other sectors of the economic system as well. Secondly, there is the existence in the economic system (save in rather exceptional periods such as war-time) of a considerable margin of excess productive capacity—of unemployed resources both of man-power and of capital equipment.

At first sight it might look as though neither of these factors had much to do with the way in which the wage-level was determined or with the ability of collective bargaining to alter this level. But if one is thinking in terms of *real* wages, it should at once become clear that the degree of monopoly in the economic system at large (i.e. in commodity markets as well as in the labour market) may exert an important influence on real wages by affecting the relation of commodity-prices to costs, and hence to wages as an element in cost.[1] If monopoly has the effect of raising the selling-prices of goods relatively to their costs, then this will have the effect of reducing the purchasing-power of any given money-wage. Conversely, if the extent of monopoly is reduced, the level of *real* wages corresponding to any given level of *money*-wages will rise. This holds true, at any rate, of the effect of monopoly on goods which are consumed by wage-earners—wage-goods as they have come to be called. Some economists even maintain that the degree of monopoly in the economic system at large is the main determinant of labour's share in the total product, and that the productivity of labour and the degree of monopoly in the industries which produce wage-goods are joint determinants of the prevailing level of real wages.

---

[1] To an over-all view of industry short-period or prime costs consist of wages plus imported raw materials ; and if one is speaking of a " closed system " (i.e. abstracting from imports and exports), all such costs are ultimately reducible to wages in some form.

In one respect it might seem to follow from this that trade-union bargaining over wages (which is usually conducted in terms of money-wages) can have little influence over labour's real share, and that the traditional *laissez-faire* view is vindicated after all, if for new reasons. But this conclusion is not necessarily correct, since trade union action can be a powerful factor in counteracting the influence that buyers' monopoly in the *labour* market can exert directly on money-wages; and to this extent it can narrow the gap between wages and commodity-prices. Moreover, if trade union action were to concern itself with the control of commodity-prices (and hence of profit-margins), as well as with the fixing of money-wages, with which trade unions have been preoccupied in the past, it would possess a much enhanced power to influence labour's share of the product.

The emphasis in recent economic theory on problems connected with the existence of unused productive capacity does not so directly impinge on the theory of wages as does the emphasis on the effects of monopoly of which we have just spoken. But it introduces several new variables among those upon which, according to traditional theory, the number of jobs forthcoming at a certain wage-level depends. In particular, it implies that the extent to which existing capital equipment is utilized, depending on the state of demand for consumption goods and for capital goods (i.e. on the amount of consumption *plus* investment), will be a principal determinant of the level of employment; and that in any situation (e.g. of technique, stock of capital and natural resources), and with any given level of wages, there may be a large number of possible levels of employment. One result of this is to cast doubt on the simple notion of some kind of elastic demand-schedule for labour, which we have seen lay at the heart of the traditional theory of wages, with its corollary that a rise in the level of money-wages would inevitably result in a contraction of employment. Moreover, this new emphasis indicates the possibility—even the probability—that if labour is successful in securing a larger share of total income, this fact may bring about an actual *increase*, instead of a decrease, in the level of employment. The reason for this rather startling conclusion is that wage-earners usually spend nearly all of any income they get (having little margin to spare beyond necessary expenditure), whereas the rich save a considerable part of their incomes. Consequently, a transfer of income from the latter to the former is likely to increase the amount *spent* out of a given total income, and hence increase the demand alike for goods and for the labour to make them.

§ 7. **How far can Wages be Raised ?**   Where then does this discussion lead us ?   Clearly the confident pessimism of early economists is gone.   The economic world faces us with too complex a situation of interacting forces to enable us to extract rigid forecasts about it from theories of the traditional type.   It is not merely that the situation is one of continual change and movement, where the " long-period " and its " equilibrium " are never reached before some fresh change intervenes : it is that the process of moving towards this long-period may generate changes which alter the character of the long-period tendency itself.   It is as though it were a question, not merely of the pendulum of a clock never having time to settle in the vertical position before it is again jerked away, but of the swing of the pendulum being powerful enough at times to shift the position of the clock itself.   Contrary to the traditional view, it may well be the case that wage-theory as we know it is better suited to short-period forecast (or at least, to some intermediate period between short and long) while for long-period forecast it is a deceptive guide.   But it is precisely short-period conditions that some of the main assumptions of the *laissez-faire* theory do not fit.

Are we then left only with a halting agnosticism, which can neither forecast nor understand? Can we see no more pattern to the labour-market than a disordered tumble of warring forces? Clearly we do not need to reach so sceptical a conclusion as this, even if we reject any rigidly deterministic view. We know many of the crucial relationships which govern the shape of events; and we shall know more of their precise nature with progress in the realistic and statistical study of actual situations of which there is so much need. We have some basis for at least provisional conclusions as to the effect of particular courses of action on particular situations—for example, of wage-changes in a particular industry; even if we can with less confidence pass from the part to the whole. But even when we are dealing with the general level of wages and with a long-run perspective, we know that there are definite limits within which the course of wages must lie.

On the one hand, the general wage-level is unlikely to fall for long below a bare physical subsistence standard—a standard which, as we have seen, is not a fixed level, since the amount of subsistence will depend on how arduous or intensive the work is; although, if plentiful new supplies of labour from outside (e.g. by immigration from rural districts or from abroad) are forthcoming, this minimum standard may be very low, sufficient only for the bare physical needs of the present, and not for maintaining a normal working-life or for rearing a family. From the figures which were quoted in Chapter II one might judge that wages in fact were not, on the average, far above this physical limit (and were in many cases below it) until quite recently at least; differences between countries apparently corresponding fairly closely to differences in work-intensity that require different subsistence-standards.

The upper limit to wages proves more difficult to define. This limit might at first seem to be simply defined by the statement that wages cannot rise so as to absorb more than that part of the surplus produce going to capitalists which is at present *spent*, since, if wages absorbed more than this, they would eat into the supply of capital. If control of all production and investment were to be taken over by the State, it is true that the share of wages in the total product could rise to this extent. Even so, this does not mean, however, that the share of wages could absorb the *whole* net product, unless there were to be no new investment in expanding the existing stock of capital. To the extent that new investment was taking place, part of the man-power and materials of the community would have to be devoted to building new factories and making and installing new machinery, instead of to manufacturing consumers' goods to go into the shops for earners to buy. Only the latter would be available to give purchasing power to wages ; and consequently the real value of the total wage-bill of the country could only amount to *part* of the (net) value of all the goods produced by labour.

It is also true and important that, if there is a substantial reserve of unused productive capacity in the economic system, both the total product and aggregate real wage-earnings could be augmented by this amount : augmented by measures to " take in the slack " and to bring into production the man-power and resources that were previously unused or underused.

But in a capitalist system, where production and investment are under the control of private owners, it would be absurd to say that the only limit to an increase in the share of wages was the amount of total income which was normally devoted to investment. In practice, under these conditions, the actual limit to any upward movement of wages is obviously lower

than this. The definition of this limit is probably much
more a matter of politics and social psychology than it is a
matter for economic theory. We have referred to the fact
that much of the possibility of a rise in real wages depends
on what happens to the conventional standards of consumption of the capitalist class. These conventional standards,
once adopted, are much slower to be revised in a downward
direction, short of some cataclysm like a war or revolution,
than they are to move in an upward direction. Habits of
country-houses and servants and grouse-moors are more
slowly abandoned than acquired. During properous periods
when the gross product of industry is expanding, wage-earners,
if strongly organized, are in a good position for raising their
wages, both in the aggregate and relatively to the share which
goes to property-owners. If strongly organized enough, they
could conceivably secure nearly the whole fruits of economic
progress ; although, as we have seen, a great deal depends
on how far, through the possession and exploitation of
monopoly-power, employers are in a position to pass on any
pressure for money-wage advances in higher prices of wage-
goods, and hence to frustrate attempts to raise real wages.
But at less prosperous times, when the total product of industry
is stationary or advancing only slowly, the power of trade
unions, however strongly organized, seems in practice to be
much more straitly limited. Attempts to raise the share of
wages at the expense of other incomes seems likely, in these
circumstances, to meet severe resistance ; and before long,
instead of pruning their standards of consumption, capitalists
will probably reduce their investment, and firms may try to
economize on labour to the maximum possible extent by
substituting labour-saving machinery. Moreover, more spec-
tacular forms of " a strike of capital " may, of course, occur.
While the workers may succeed in improving the rate at which
they barter effort against earnings, and raise the relative

share of wages in the total product so far as trade union action is capable of reducing the degree of monopoly, their power to increase total earnings in these circumstances will probably not be very great, short of more sweeping institutional changes in the economic system itself.

CHAPTER VI

WAGE DIFFERENCES

§ 1. Differences between Grades. Hitherto we have dealt with the size of total wages in the community and with the *general* level of wages on the average ; and we have ignored quite wide differences which are found, both in wages per hour and per piece, between different grades of workers, and between different districts and industries inside the same country, as well as between different nations of the world. But an important, if subordinate, half of the theory of wages has always dealt with the causes of wage-differences ; and in the practical problem of wage-regulation this question of particular wages occupies a prominent place.

We have seen in Chapter I that for everyone in actual fact (as well as nominally) to have an equal choice of taking to any occupation he pleased, the character of the economic system would have to be fundamentally different from what it is. Let us imagine, however, that inside the category of wage-occupations—leaving other classes of income on one side—this equality of choice was realized, and that everyone had an approximately equal chance of adopting any employment that he pleased. Under these conditions one would not expect wage-rates everywhere to be identical : they would differ for several clear and definite reasons. But one would expect them to differ only by so much as would leave what Adam Smith called " the advantages and disadvantages " of various occupations equal. This *Principle of Equal Net Advantages* would tend to be realized as a result of the movement of labour from one occupation to another, as the level of water in two cisterns tends to equality if they are connected

138

by an adequate pipe. If one trade seemed on balance to be preferable to another, after all the advantages, including the wages to be earned, had been measured against its disadvantages, workers would then tend to move into the one and to shun the other, until the shifting of supply, by altering the relative wage-levels, had equalized the net advantages of the two trades. Wages would then tend to differ only to the extent of differences in the disagreeableness or the cost of various occupations. To quote Adam Smith's own words: "The whole of the advantages and disadvantages of the different employments of labour and stock must, in the same neighbourhood, be either perfectly equal, or continually tending to equality. If in the same neighbourhood there was any employment evidently either more or less advantageous than the rest, so many people would crowd into it in the one case, and so many would desert it in the other, that its advantages would soon return to the level of other employments." [1]

In the first place, for example, one would expect people to shun the more disagreeable or the more dangerous occupations like sewage-work or coal-mining unless the wages in those trades were sufficiently higher than elsewhere to offset this extra disagreeableness or danger. The result of this common dislike for cleaning sewers or hewing coal would be to make applicants for employment in those trades more scarce than elsewhere ; and this very scarcity would tend to raise the wages in sewers and mines. Similar considerations would apply to an occupation which involved a greater chance of unemployment or wide uncertainty of earnings. On the other hand, if certain trades were particularly pleasant or interesting, or carried with them some special social distinction or prestige, or special privileges or chances of advancement, one would expect popular preference to flood these trades

[1] *Wealth of Nations*, Ed. 1826, p. 99.

with applicants for employment and cause labour there to be cheaper than elsewhere.

Secondly, people would be likely to shun those employments which required a costly education or training or a long period of probation or apprenticeship during which nothing was earned ; and this would tend to raise wages in those employments until they were higher than elsewhere. The expenditure on the preliminary training would then be in the nature of a capital outlay which would only be undertaken if the higher wage to be gained in the future seemed to make the outlay worth while.

One might, further, expect employments which required some scarce natural aptitude, such as those of jockeys or opera singers or steeplejacks, to offer an abnormally high wage because of the keen competition to secure the services of the limited number of persons suitable to fulfil them. But in this case the favoured persons would not be merely receiving something which compensated some extra disadvantage in their employment : they would be in a privileged position in which the total advantages of their occupation (in Adam Smith's phrase) were greater than elsewhere ; and they could be considered as receiving an exceptional type of " scarcity-price " or " rent " of a scarce natural quality.

In the actual system under which we live " equality of net advantages " is very far from being realized (i.e. even within the category of work-incomes, apart from incomes on property). Moreover the extent to which wages vary more widely than the advantages and disadvantages of different occupations is considerably greater than can be reasonably explained by the final cause that we have mentioned. So much do actual wage-differences run in conflict with this principle as to incline one to think that it cannot be an explanation at all of the major differences of wages in our present wage-system. The unpleasant work of the community is among the lowest paid rather than the most highly paid, as is also most of the work involving danger to health and life. Low wages are generally combined with fluctuating and inconstant employment ; and the level of incomes in skilled occupations and trained professions is generally higher by much more than can reasonably be ascribed to interest on capital laid out in the preliminary training. It has been suggested that, if a policy of maintaining full employment were to be successfully operated, one result would be a drastic transformation of relative earnings in different occupations ; since if jobs were as plentiful as job-seekers, people would shun the disagreeable and dangerous jobs, until the competition of employers to get hold of enough labour to fill these jobs forced wages in them to several times their previous level. Some indication of this possibility has been seen in the acute scarcity of coal-miners after the Second World War. In a society without unemployment and with a greater approach to equality of opportunity coal-miners, foundry-workers and refuse-collectors might be among the best-paid people, and sedentary workers in comfortable offices among the lowest paid. A job that made the hands dirty might bring both high pay and high social esteem, and a job that could be done with clean hands might come to be regarded as a " soft option " requiring a relatively meagre reward. At any rate, some other explanation of our existing topsy-turvy wage-differences than the principle of equal net advantages is evidently needed.

§ 2. " Non-Competing Groups ". This further explanation is supplied as soon as we remove the artificial assumption that every wage-earner has an equal chance of entering any occupation. In actuality this is far from being the case. The chief reason lies in the fact that differences of income once established are apt to perpetuate themselves in a world where the cost of training for an occupation is an expense which the individual wage-earner has to find out of his own pocket. Those who possess a higher income, and perhaps have some savings in reserve as well, will be better able to bear the cost of training and apprenticeship for their children to enter a skilled occupation ; whereas the unskilled labourer who can with difficulty feed his family may be unable to bear the cost at all. A moderately well-to-do unskilled worker's family usually tries to apprentice the eldest son to a skilled trade. But it can rarely do more than this ; and once this effort has been made, the younger sons usually have to take whatever work yields immediate earnings as soon as they leave school.[1] It is this fact that the supply-conditions of different grades of labour are so largely affected by the prevailing wage-differences between those grades, which is apt to make any attempt to talk about " fair " or " normal " wages of one grade relatively to another an argument in a circle. It may even produce the paradoxical result that a narrowing of the gap between skilled and unskilled wages (if it involves a rise in unskilled wages) will actually *increase* the supply of skilled labour, thereby precipitating a further narrowing of the gap. In the so-called " middle class professions " this influence will be particularly marked : here the potential supply of lawyers or doctors or university teachers will be almost entirely confined (apart from scholarships and acts of charity) to children of parents above the income-level of manual wage-earners. Accordingly, the supply of entrants to these professions will be specially limited, and the level of income will be raised by reason of this limitation. On the other hand, little more than a modicum of physical strength is required to work as a docker or a navvy, and the supply available for such employments is consequently plentiful and cheap. Professor Taussig has suggested that five distinct grades can

[1] Cf. E. L. Lewis, *The Children of the Unskilled*, pp. 15–16.

be distinguished; the passage from the lower into the next higher one being in each case particularly hampered by various circumstances. The higher grades constitute what he terms (following Cairnes) " non-competing groups "— that is, groups in which supply is particularly limited because of the restricted entry of persons from outside. And since the supply of persons available for these groups of occupations is limited, the price which their services can command tends to be raised. The grades which he distinguishes are: first, unskilled workers like general labourers; second, semi-skilled workers; third, skilled craftsmen, such as mechanics, fitters, locomotive-drivers, bricklayers; fourth, clerical workers; fifth the various " middle-class professions ". The privileged position of this latter grade is, indeed, sufficiently great to remove it from the class of wage-earners as we defined it in Chapter I, and to place it in a category apart.

The privileged income which a particular grade can enjoy will be further increased if artificial restrictions are imposed on newcomers entering a trade, either by law or custom or the regulations of some association, since these restrictions will further limit the number of persons able to compete with the members of this trade for employment. It was the practice of mediæval gilds, at least in their later days, to limit competition among themselves by imposing entrance qualifications on their members; and some of the more powerful of them eventually became highly exclusive, levying entrance fees which amounted to several hundred pounds. In the last century some trade unions among skilled craftsmen (see Chapter VII) limited entrance to their trade; and limitation in the form of fairly strict apprenticeship regulations still exists. Bar fees, the customs connected with a solicitor's " articles ", the price of a share in a broker's business exercise a similar influence; while some professions virtually confine their selection to those who hail from a certain number of select public schools, and others demand a certain standard of social deportment and speech.

But existing wage-differences may not only affect the supply of labour in different grades by their influence on the number of people who can afford the cost of training; they may also do so by their influence on conventional notions as to what is and is not a "disagreeable" trade. Probably wage-differences by themselves have only a minor influence on such conventions, which are mainly the product of wider inequalities between classes. At any rate, there is evidently a tendency, in class societies, for occupations which have traditionally been poorly paid to be considered disagreeable and for those carrying a higher income to be considered more socially respectable or honourable. The effect of this influence would be to increase the "upward mobility" of labour, and to make people anxious to enter the higher grades even at considerable sacrifice to themselves; but it is usually overborne by the influence of the other factors that we have mentioned. It may, however, serve to explain why some occupations which lie just above the manual worker grades and which involve some, though not a very large, cost of training, are sufficiently flooded with entrants to depress their wages in many cases below those of many skilled manual workers: for example, clerical workers and teachers; and why there is at this point rather more "upward mobility" than one might expect.

§ 3. **Differences between Industries and Districts.** Obstacles to movement may exist, not only horizontally (so to speak) between grades of labour, but vertically between different industries or between different localities; and this will tend to cause what some economists have termed "unfairness" of wages as between localities and industries—"unfair" in the purely relative sense that labour is paid less (or more) in one place than labour of equivalent skill and efficiency elsewhere. These obstacles may take the form of ignorance as to the existence of jobs in another town or industry, of the lack of means to move both home and family to a distant place, or of unwillingness for various reasons to leave a familiar trade, coupled with an optimism that " something will sooner or later turn up ". It is often said that the housing shortage of recent years has seriously reduced the mobility of labour from place to place, because a worker who has a house or rooms is loath to forsake them for the prospect of homelessness elsewhere. Where movement is sluggish for any of these reasons, labour may be relatively abundant in some towns or trades at the same time as it is quite scarce in others ; and this may cause wages to fall in the former and to rise in the latter, until the gap between the two is sufficiently great to encourage at any rate some movement of workers between the two. It may further happen that, when there is little movement of workers between two trades or places, the " supply-price " at which workers are willing to offer their labour may differ quite widely, so that the wage-level is lower where labour, either by custom or because of poverty, places a high valuation on money-income in terms of what it is willing to do and to forgo in return. The relative lowness of wages in agriculture, for instance, has usually been attributed in large part to the tardiness with which villagers move off to improve their fortunes in the towns.

To the extent that these obstacles to movement are geographical in character, differences in wages for the same class of work will tend to arise between different districts of the same industry—for instance, different coalfields, or agriculture in the north and the south—as much as between industries which are localized apart. To the extent that the obstacles are occupational in character differences in wages may arise between different trades even in the same town, as

L

those between the " sheltered " and " unsheltered " trades
of which mention was made in Chapter II.   In the inter-war
period there was only a limited tendency for labour to move
from the misery of South Wales mining valleys to compete
for employment among better-paid builders or transport
workers in the South of England, or to move from shipbuilding
into neighbouring trades which were better paid.   In addition
to the reasons that have been already mentioned, this may
be largely due to the fact that to-day when wages are fixed
by trade union agreement there is less chance of workers
undercutting those already employed by offering themselves
at a cheaper rate ; while it is also probably true that workers
are more likely to be induced to move by the offer of new
openings and rising wages in expanding trades than they are
by the harsh pressure of falling wages and unemployment
in their old accustomed trade and place of birth—in other
words, mobility of labour is probably greater on a rising
than on a falling labour market.

§ 4. " Casual " Employment.   Such immobility of labour is
likely to be enhanced by anything which encourages the hope
that " something will turn up " in the old trade, when actually
there is no longer sufficient work available there to afford
constant employment to the same number of workers as
before.   And this hope that " something will turn up " which
keeps men hanging about the fringe of the trade instead of
moving off in search of better prospects elsewhere will be
materially affected by the methods of engagement which the
employers use.   If an employer staffs his factory with a regular
number of " hands " whom he employs fairly constantly from
week to week and only changes for specific reasons, the worker
who is dismissed will know that for the time being at any
rate there is " nothing doing ".   But if the employer is in
the habit of changing his staff, or a part of it, frequently—

taking on temporary workers at particular seasons, employing workers for a specific job, discharging them and hiring a new set of hands for the next job—then the situation is different. The discharged worker will feel that there are opportunities of being re-engaged, at least for a temporary period, in the near future. Those who hang on the fringe of the trade will have some chance of getting employment some of the time, even if they have little or no chance of getting employment in that trade all of the time. The extreme case of the " casual method " of employment, as it is called, used to be found in such work as unloading cargoes at the docks, where dockers were taken on, not for regular employment, but for the loading and unloading of a particular cargo and then discharged.[1] This tended to encourage a considerable " reserve of labour " to hang about the industry, much in excess of the number which could secure regular employment on the average. However many men were at the dockgates, each had equal chance with another of securing employment ; and consequently a larger number tended to gather there than were likely to be taken on at one time even on the busiest day. In such trades not only may the average earnings of a worker be unduly low because of the inconstancy of his employment, but the keen competition for work may depress wage-rates as well. Moreover, any attempts to raise these rates, while casual methods of employment remain, may merely attract a larger reserve of labour to the industry, so that average earnings are reduced rather than raised.

§ 5. The " Sweated Trades ". The problem of what is known as the " sweated trades " is a special case of wages being

---

[1] This system of employment was radically altered by the measures of " decasualization " during the Second World War—measures which were made permanent by the Dock Workers (Regulation of Employment) Act of 1946.

" unfairly " low. A " sweated trade " was defined originally by a Select Committee of the House of Lords as being characterized by " inadequate wages, inordinately long hours and insanitary conditions of labour ". In many cases these so-called " sweated trades " consisted of hand-work done in the home or in small workshops, such as paper box making, hand-made lace, some chain-making and laundry work and cheap tailoring, of which a good deal was heard before the First World War. Often it was only the possibility of acquiring supplies of cheap labour which apparently kept these trades and their existing methods alive : otherwise the work would presumably have been done by machine methods in more up-to-date factories. Like parasites, accordingly, these trades tended to fasten on to those areas where supplies of cheap labour were obtainable. In the majority of cases this cheap labour was women's labour, driven by the death or illness or unemployment of the male breadwinner to earn some supplement to the family earnings. If the workers in question had been sufficiently well informed, or less urgently in need of immediate earnings, and had been able to move in search of alternative employment elsewhere, they would not have accepted these exceptionally low rates. Sometimes it was the case, therefore, that if an attempt had been made to forbid the payment of these " sweated " rates, the trades could hardly have survived in competition with better-equipped machine industry—cheap labour acted as a subsidy to their inefficiency ; and in this case the workers concerned would have suffered complete loss of earnings in unemployment. Solution, to be complete, has to achieve the transfer of the surplus labour elsewhere. The whole problem is merely a particular illustration of the tendency of poverty to breed poverty which was referred to in the last chapter. It is often the poverty of male wage-earners which compels the women members of the family to go out and seek employment, and so enables the " sweated trades " to thrive on the supply of cheap labour thereby created ; and once the price of labour falls substantially, its supply-price is likely to be reduced, so that worse terms of employment are readily accepted in the future.

§ 6. **Men's and Women's Wages.** To a large extent the problem of " sweated " labour is only an extreme case of the general problem of male and female labour and their respective wages—although, of course, there may be, and is, " sweating " among men as well as among women workers. If men and women could never be substituted for one another on the same job, male and female labour would constitute a pure case of " non-competing groups ", in Cairnes's sense that transfer from one group to the other was not possible. It might happen, of course, that a woman cook pretended to be a Paris *chef* or a man disguised himself as a nursemaid or a governess ; but such devices are not apparently very frequent. One would then expect the price of labour in the two groups to differ if conditions of supply and demand in one group were different from those in the other. On the side of demand there is the fact that there may be fewer remunerative jobs for which women are as fully suited as are men. In some cases women will be definitely superior, as in certain operations of cotton-spinning or in teaching small children ; while for heavy muscular operations like coal-hewing and iron-moulding women will clearly be unsuited. It is sometimes said that, because women are more liable to illness or only to apply themselves temporarily to an employment, they may be less useful to an employer for this reason alone. Added to this is the probable effect of custom in excluding women from some occupations.

The average difference, however, between the level of men's and women's wages is in most countries nearly as much as

50 per cent—a difference which seems considerably greater than can be attributed to factors on the demand side alone. The following table [1] shows the position in various countries as it existed in the period between the wars.

	Nature of Statistics.	Date.	Ratio of Women's to Men's Wage (Men's Wage = 100).
Australia . .	Weekly rates	Sept. 30, 1925	53
Denmark . .	Hourly earnings	4th. qr., 1925	58
France . .	Daily rates	Oct. 1924	52
Britain . .	Trade Board hourly minima	Jan. 1, 1926	56
Sweden . .	Hourly earnings	1924	61
U.S.A. . .	Weekly earnings	June 1925	59
New York .	Weekly earnings	April 1926	56
Massachusetts	Weekly earnings	May 1926	57

In explaining the wideness of this difference the conditions of supply of female labour probably play a decisive part. If the supply-price of women's labour is generally lower than that of men, this by itself would suffice to explain the lower rates paid in women's trades. This in fact seems to be the case. It is true that an unmarried woman who goes out to work does so as a rule either to earn " pin-money " or to add something to the family earnings at home, and the smaller urgency of her need might seem likely to *raise* the supply-price of her labour—to make her unwilling to go out to work unless the inducement was fairly high. In some cases this is probably so ; for example, it clearly applies to middle-class women ;

---

[1] Cited from J. H. Richardson, *The Minimum Wage*, p. 136.

and it might be the case that if employers sought to extend their employment of unmarried women at all considerably, the price offered to female labour would have to be increased a good deal. At the same time, it seems probable that the influence of custom, and the desire for independence among young unmarried women, operates in the other direction and may well counteract the effect of the lesser urgency to secure employment. Precisely because young women are unaccustomed to earning and value independence, they may place a higher value on the acquisition of a few shillings than other people do. Of decisive influence, however, on the supply of women in the labour market is probably the number of women who seek employment because their family is in straitened circumstances through the low earnings, unemployment, illness or death of the male breadwinner. These women, since they are driven to work only by the pressure of poverty, may be ready to work for almost anything they can get, and they will value low immediate earnings, even though spasmodic and temporary, more highly than future prospects which are better and surer. And for this very reason that the supply of female labour of this kind tends to vary inversely with the earnings of male labour, there will be a cumulative tendency for anything which depresses men's wages to cheapen the supply of female labour, and so (in so far as women can be substituted for men) to lower by their competition the wages of male labour still further.

But in so far as male and female labour can be substituted for one another in certain cases, they do not constitute a pure case of " non-competing groups " : although *persons* cannot change from one group to the other and so compete with the latter, the *demand for their services* can be (partially) transferred. The question at once arises : if such substitution is possible, why does it not continue until male and female wages are proportional to their relative efficiencies at the margin [1] at which the substitution is being carried out? Yet there is reason to think that this is not the case. If, therefore, women's labour is cheap relatively to its efficiency, why is not substitution of female for male labour carried out until this relative cheapness disappears? It is to be noted that this condition of wages proportional to relative efficiencies, which one might expect competition to produce, does not necessarily mean an equality of *time-rates* between the two classes of labour. But one might expect it to yield an *approximate* equality of *piece-rates* for men and women; since then, if male workers were capable of producing more in a given time than female workers, this difference of output would be reflected in a proportional difference of earnings.

Two reasons have been suggested to explain why this equality (or approach to equality) is not realized. First, it has been pointed out that the substitution of women for men is limited fairly narrowly and often could not be extended either without a considerable breach with custom or without special cost. It has been estimated that only a fifth of the male workers are engaged in trades in which women are also employed; while, as Mr. and Mrs. Webb have said, " even in the industries which employ both men and women we nearly always find the sexes sharply divided in different departments, working at different processes and performing different operations ", and " in the vast majority of cases these several departments, processes and operations are mutually complementary, and there is no question of sex rivalry ".[2] Custom probably plays a considerable part in making employers reluctant to teach a trade to women, and so in setting a barrier against the invasion of women, even

---

[1] Seeing that there are some trades at which men are unquestionably superior to women and some at which women are unquestionably superior to men, there will be no tendency for the wages to be proportional to the difference of efficiency on the *average* of all trades (if this can be given a meaning).   [2] *Industrial Democracy*, Ed. 1919, p. 496.

where, if tested, women might prove as suitable as men. Moreover, male trade unions in the past have commonly made strenuous attempts to exact agreements with employers which have the effect of stemming the intrusion of women workers, or even of excluding them altogether, whenever serious danger seemed to exist of male standards being undercut by the competition of cheaper female labour. The very tendency of substitution to establish an equality of efficiency-wages accordingly evokes resistances to stem its further operation.

The second reason that has been suggested is that in any given locality the supply-curve of women's labour, after a point, becomes distinctly inelastic, in the sense that a steadily rising price would have to be offered to attract additional quantities of women's labour into the labour market. This is for the reason that at any one time there is a fairly fixed number of women who for the various reasons we have described decide to take up employment.[1] Special circumstances are necessary to swell their ranks in any appreciable numbers from among those who usually stay at home and attend to domestic duties. This inelasticity of supply beyond a point, when combined with the fact that competition between employers for labour is imperfect, will result in the wages of those in employment remaining low and employers being reluctant to extend their employment of women for fear of this increased demand for female labour raising the price of this labour all-round to their own disadvantage. If these conditions prevail, then female labour will be abnormally exploited, and any tendencies to raise women's wages by extending the demand for women will be blunted. It will be left for long-term shifts in industry, tardily and uncertainly, to effect any considerable substitution of women

---

[1] Evidence in support of this view was advanced by Professor Sargent Florence in *The Economic Journal* for March, 1931.

for men. But even of this long-term shift there is no great evidence.

§ 7. " Equal Pay for Equal Work." It has frequently been urged that, in order both to do justice to women workers and to remove the danger to male workers of being undercut and supplanted by female competition, the principle of " Equal Pay for Equal Work "—in other words, equal piece-rates for workers of equal capabilities—should be adopted in all trades where men and women compete for employment. In cases where women were less useful to an employer than men this would, of course, tend to have the effect of closing the trade to women altogether, since an employer would not employ a woman at the same price in preference to the more useful man ; and in so far as this occurred the tendency would be to lower the general level of female wages by confining the demand for women to a smaller number of trades. Where, however, there was no marked disparity between the suitability of the two sexes for the trade, the adoption of the principle might have an opposite effect. By removing the fear of male trade unionists that they were subject to unfair competition it might induce them to relax or remove some of their restrictions on the entry of women, and thereby result in the admission of women to certain trades from which they were formerly excluded. At any rate, it is clear that there is considerable room for the extension of trade union organization among women, where it has hitherto been but weak or even non-existent, which would have the effect of raising the female wage-level by collective bargaining both in exclusively women's trades and also in trades where women compete with men. From the point of view of the male trade unionist such organization of a weaker section of wage-earners cannot fail to be beneficial, in so far as the two are competitors for employment. How far this, or the establishment of the principle of " Equal

Pay for Equal Work ", is likely to increase the aggregate earnings of the working class all round depends on the issues discussed in Chapter V. Both amount to a raising of the " supply-curve " for a particular section of wage-earners, namely women. If the higher female wage has the effect of improving working efficiency at all considerably, these measures of improvement will almost certainly increase earnings all round. But whether it does this or not, it will improve the position of labour in so far as it enables the working class as a whole to get more in proportion to the energy it expends.

§ 8. **International Wage-differences.** When we come to enquire the reason of the wide differences of wages between different countries, such as those detailed in Chapter II, we shall find that similar considerations apply as in the case of wage-variations between different districts within the same country. In the first place it is important to remember that money-wages may differ considerably even while real wages remain the same. Money-wages are frequently higher in large urban areas than in small country towns, as for instance in the case of printers, a large part of the difference being balanced by the different cost of living in the countryside and in the large town. The difficulty of comparing real wages between different countries and the possibility of errors in current estimates of them have already been referred to in Chapter II ; but it is the level of real wages in different countries that for most purposes is the significant thing on which we need to fasten attention.[1] Secondly, it is necessary to compare both the

---

[1] For some purposes, of course, differences of money-wages between two countries may be the relevant consideration. For instance, let us suppose that two countries have equal levels of real wages, but for some reason this co-exists with a difference in *money*-wages between the two (i.e. in terms of gold at the prevailing rate of exchange) ; then the employers in the low-money-wage country would be at a relative advantage and

real wages and also the relative skill and efficiency of labour in the two districts or countries concerned. Differences in wages between town and country or between one district and another—for instance, between the North of England and the South—may not be " unfair " in a relative sense, because they correspond to equivalent differences in efficiency and skill. Similarly, the cotton operative of Bombay or Shanghai works less skilfully and intensively than the cotton operative of Bolton or Oldham, and the difference in labour-cost to an employer is considerably less than would appear from a mere comparison of the real wage. At the same time it may quite well be true that the low efficiency of the low-paid worker is an effect as much as a cause of his low standard of life : the Bombay operative is fitted as little by his diet and housing conditions as by custom and upbringing for highly intensive factory work. What is relevant at the moment is that a competitive system establishes no tendency in this case for real wages to be equal, and we have no reason to be surprised if they are not so.

International differences of real wages, however, probably exist on a considerably greater scale than differences of working skill and efficiency ; and differences of this kind, between countries as inside a country, can only persist in so far as movement both of labour and the demand for it—in other words, of capital—is hindered, and the economic systems of different countries constitute " non-competing groups ". In this respect labour is probably less mobile than is capital. A certain amount of immigration into high-wage countries takes place ; and if the difference in wage-levels is sufficiently great, the flow may become quite large. Throughout the last hundred

the employers in the high-money-wage country at a relative disadvantage where production for export was concerned. This is said to have been an important consideration which influenced cotton manufacturers of a century ago to advocate the repeal of import duties on corn.

years there has been a steady stream of emigrants from Europe
to U.S.A.   Nevertheless such movement of labour is restrained
and limited by various factors—by the poverty of the workers
themselves, by difficulties of language and citizenship and
custom, and by the natural inertia which persuades the
average man to prefer the accustomed to the speculative and
the unknown. Not very many French or German workers
come to work in Lancashire because the promise of employment there is brighter : still less do Indians and Chinese,
save in specific cases such as seamen on British ships.
And should immigration attain sufficient dimensions to
undermine the standard of the higher-wage country, immigration restrictions on the entry of aliens, as in U.S.A., Australia,
and Britain, are likely to be imposed.

Just as inside a country, therefore, a particular grade of
labour may possess a privileged position and constitute a sort
of " aristocracy of labour ", so the wage-earners of a country
that is particularly rich in natural or acquired advantages,
or more industrially advanced than its neighbours, may share
some of the differential prosperity of their masters and constitute a kind of " aristocracy of labour " with regard to the
rest of the world. And here custom and past tradition may
play an important part. In countries where low wages have
ruled custom will tend to cause the supply-price of labour
to remain low, and hence to perpetuate an exceptionally low
level of relative wages and of real wages ; while in countries
where labour at some time or other has been able to secure
a larger share, either relative or absolute, of the produce,
this very fact, by influencing both the supply-price of labour
and the habits and valuations of the employing and investing
class, may be the principal reason for the wage-level continuing
to remain high.

In modern times, however, capital has shown an increasing
tendency to move across national boundaries particularly since

the growth of modern imperialism has extended the political domination of advanced capitalist countries over the less developed countries of the earth. In some cases political policy has definitely encouraged this movement of capital, as in the case of the listing of certain colonial securities under the British Trustee Acts. Just as the difference of wages between skilled and unskilled workers tends to be narrowed in so far as the latter can be substituted for the former in the same jobs, so this transferred demand for labour from the high-wage to the low-wage countries tends to undermine the privileged position of the " aristocracy of labour " in the more developed countries. If this movement of capital continued unhindered, it would tend towards an equality of wages the world over for labour of similar efficiency and skill ; and in so far as working efficiency itself is influenced by the standard of life, the movement of capital might tend to level-up many of the differences of efficiency as well. No such unlimited movement of capital, of course, exists. But sufficient movement has taken place in recent times to threaten quite seriously the higher wage standards of the more privileged sections of the working class in England and the U.S.A. In the U.S.A. one has witnessed the much-talked-of " transfer of industry " to the Southern States, where labour tends to be cheaper, which is paralleled by the tendency for European capital to flow into India, China and Japan, South America and Australasia, and to develop industry there which competes with the older established industries of Europe. While it is true that in the past the " aristocracy of labour " in the higher-wage countries have received compensating benefits in the shape of the cheaper food and raw materials which the opening up of new countries by foreign investment has made possible, the threat to their standards from the competing attractions of low-wage areas is to-day of no mean importance ; and here, as with any case of competition from cheaper strata of labour, the wage-earners of Europe and U.S.A. stand to benefit from an extension of organization or any similar change which raises the supply-price of their Asiatic brethren.

CHAPTER VII

TRADE UNIONISM AND WAGES

§ 1. The Character of Trade Unions. Trade unions are essentially the product of a capitalist wage-system in that they represent the obvious line of defence against the economic weakness in which propertyless wage-earners find themselves when acting as unorganized individuals. Their essential function is to overcome this weakness by substituting a *collective bargain* for separate individual bargaining; thereby both raising the supply-price at which labour is sold and making the rate of wages uniform over a whole trade. Some persons have claimed to find in trade unions a parallel, if not an actual historical connection, with the mediæval craft gilds. But this view has little reason to support it. It is now generally agreed that in so far as trade unions have any recognizable parentage, this is to be traced to the associations of journeymen, or day labourers, which appeared spasmodically in the fifteenth and sixteenth centuries whenever germs of a distinctively wage-earning class were found, rather than to the craft or mercantile gilds. The latter were essentially associations of master-craftsmen, who both produced and sold commodities and often themselves employed journeymen as well as apprentices. In later times many of them came to be associations exclusively of traders, in many ways resembling the sales associations of the present day. A trade union, on the other hand, is an association of a class of persons in a peculiar social and economic position, concerned in bargaining over the sale of labour and the conditions of employment; and since labour-power as a commodity has certain special features, which have been discussed in previous chapters, confusion rather than clarity seems to be the likely result of identifying a trade union with an ordinary sales association.

§ 2. The Beginnings of Trade Unionism. While there is evidence that combinations of handicraftsmen, with aims similar to a trade union's, appeared in the eighteenth century (for instance, among London tailors as early as 1720, and later among curriers, farriers, coach-makers and silk-weavers), trade unionism can be said to have had its beginning with the rapid spread of factory industry at the beginning of the nineteenth century. The earlier combinations seem to have been mainly spasmodic in character, and to have been found among crafts-men who were already in a semi-dependent and semi-pro-letarian condition ; and it was not until the growth of a substantial factory wage-earning class that there was soil for trade unionism, as a permanent institution, to strike root. These early trade unions were generally local trade clubs and societies, often quite small in number, and composed of select groups of skilled artisans who prided themselves on being a privileged " aristocracy " within the ranks of the working class. Many of them used the customs and ritual of the old secret societies, and elaborate initiation ceremonies were common. We find bodies like the Phœnix Society of Painters in London expecting its members to attend meetings in frock-coats and top-hats. The Manchester Order of Bricklayers excluded " any member found fighting " and maintained rules against " wrestling, leaping, racing, football, acts of bravado, drunkenness or immoral conduct ", while another society excluded any " drunkard, swearer or Sabbath-breaker ".[1] At the same time there were the beginnings of a mass type of unionism : for example, among the pitmen on the Tyne in the 'twenties and 'thirties under Thomas Hepburn, and in the 'thirties among agricultural labourers and Lancashire spinners.

[1] R. W. Postgate, *The Builders' History*, pp. 18 and 32.

M

Banned as illegal conspiracies by the law until 1824, when the Combination Acts were repealed, and even after this repeal persecuted in numerous ways under the common law and refused recognition by employers, their methods were more often direct action than negotiation ; and while the masters called in the police and military and (where they could) evicted strikers from their homes, the workers on their side often resorted to sabotage and violence. During the 1830's there were ambitious attempts to link up these local trade clubs by federation into larger national organizations, of which the Federation of Cotton Spinners, the Builders' Union and Robert Owen's grandiose scheme of the single Grand National Consolidated Trades Union were the chief. But so long as the basis of organization remained local and sectional, with the personnel of each local union possessed of no wider horizon than that of its own town and dominated primarily by specific group interests, wider federations were bound to lack cohesion. And it was not until a group of far-looking trade union leaders succeeded in building strong national unions with centralized finances in the 'fifties and 'sixties out of the heterogeneous local trade clubs, that the main lines of modern trade union organization were laid. These new unions were at the time called " The New Model " ; but later in the century came to be called in retrospect " The Old Unionism ".

§ 3. The " Old Unionism ". These new national " amalgamated " unions, of which the Amalgamated Society of Engineers, formed in 1850, was the model, while they were national in scope, remained like the old trade clubs essentially organizations of the superior skilled craftsmen which did not admit or cater for the lower unskilled grades. Cautious and conservative in outlook, and in general rejecting the strike weapon in favour of the establishment of joint negotiating boards with the employers and of conciliation and arbitration, they

aimed to secure for themselves a privileged position in the
labour market by making their labour scarce. Their methods
were virtually the monopolist measures of the old gilds,
designed to make their craft more securely into a "non-
competing group" and so to sell their services at a higher
price. This "fundamental principle" of their policy was
clearly enunciated by one union, the Flint Glassmakers, in an
address of the Executive in 1857 : "It is simply a question
of supply and demand, and we all know that if we supply
a greater quantity of an article than what is actually demanded
the cheapening of that article, whether it be labour or any
other commodity, is the natural result." "You keep your
own wages good," said the retiring secretary in a farewell
address in 1854, "by the simple act of clearing the surplus
labour out of the market." [1] Many of the old local trade
clubs had used methods of this kind, which the new amalgamated unions now took over and used on a national scale.
The Dublin Coopers and the Cork Stonemasons had the
custom until recently of levying a tax of 1s. a week on all
" outsiders " coming to seek employment from another town.
Half of this amount went into a special fund for the purpose
of paying the return fare for " outsiders " and sending them
out of the town as soon as trade slackened and any danger
of unemployment appeared. The national craft unions pur-
sued the same sectional objects principally by careful regulations concerning apprenticeship, which had the effect of
limiting entry to the trade, and by exacting agreements from
employers which provided for careful demarcation of the
work, both between one craft and another (as between
plumbers and fitters or joiners and patternmakers) and between craftsmen and less skilled men, thereby " earmarking "
demand for members of the particular union and preventing
the transfer of demand for their services to other workers.

[1] Cit. Webb, *History of Trade Unionism*, Ed. 1920, p. 201.

Originally the limitation of apprentices had been sanctioned by law under the old Statute of Apprentices. But this situation was terminated in 1814 ; and the early craft unions were merely continuing a custom which had formerly been enforced by law. The Stonemasons limited—and still limit—the number to one apprentice for every five or six men working, and exacted an apprenticeship period of five to seven years. The Flint Glassmakers allowed one for every six workmen ; the Lithographic Printers one for every five with a maximum of six in any firm ; while some of the Sheffield cutlery trades limited apprenticeship to sons of existing craftsmen. Among compositors the rules still vary from town to town ; but it is quite common for a rigid maximum to be placed on the number of apprentices that can be taken by any one firm. In addition, the craft unions often attempted to restrict the working of overtime ; they strengthened the economic position of their members by building large reserves in the shape of Friendly Benefit funds for use in case of sickness, accident, unemployment, or old age ; while in several cases they maintained an emigration fund, as was done by the Flint Glassmakers, the Compositors, the Bookbinders, the Ironmoulders, and the Engineers, in order to ship surplus members of the craft overseas.

These methods mark the nearest approach of trade unions in character to the old gild or the modern sales association or cartel. But with the growing invasion of the factory by machine-methods, narrowing the domain of the old handicraftsman, the power of craft unions to maintain their privileged position gradually waned. The demand for special skill contracted, as this skill was required over a narrowing field. The training required to mind a machine, however complicated, was less than was formerly needed to equip a millwright or a lithographic printer ; and to-day the skilled worker is more generally a mere responsible operator of a

complex machine-process than an artisan who has learned to
fashion material with his hands. The old stringent apprenticeship rules, as a result, had to be relaxed or abandoned, or
else they were automatically circumvented by " progression
(or promotion) within the trade ". Printing establishments
in towns where apprenticeship limitations are severe often
fill vacancies by drawing compositors from country firms
where the apprenticeship regulations do not apply or are not
enforced ; while in a modern engineering shop there exists a
gradation of different machines from the simplest, operated
by the least experienced semi-skilled hand, up to the more
complex operations requiring skill and experience. Between
any of these processes it is very hard to draw a frontier-line
to distinguish where skilled work begins and semi-skilled
operations end ; and in practice unskilled workers by passing
from one process to the other can gradually acquire the
necessary skill for the higher processes without a formal
apprenticeship, and are in fact to an increasing extent pro-
moted in this way. Consequently, the gild-like practices of
the Old Unionism are now largely obsolete. They still survive
in a few trades—the boiler-makers, the Sheffield cutlery trades,
sections of the building trades are instances. But in trades
like engineering and printing the passage of events is rendering
them less and less important ; while in a large number of
trades, such as textiles and mining and transport, they do
not exist.

§ 4. The " New Unionism ". In the last twenty years of the
nineteenth century a new wave of trade union organization,
known as the " New Unionism ", appeared. Twenty years
previously a speaker at a conference of the Working Men's
International had suggested that the growth of craft unions
might create a " fifth estate "—the outcast unskilled workers
—beneath the " fourth estate " of the organized skilled

artisans. This had to some extent occurred, and might have occurred still more noticeably had not the progress of the machine sapped much of the economic foundation for a privileged estate of skilled craftsmen. At any rate, it was precisely to this so-called " fifth estate " that the New Unionism appealed—to the masses of low-paid " unshorn chins and fustian jackets " who had been left outside the gates of the Old Unionism ; and the growth of a number of new " general labour " unions at this period, such as the Dockers' Union, the Workers' Union, the Gasworkers', the Seamen's Union and the National Union of General and Municipal Workers, represented the first comprehensive attempt of the unskilled workers to organize themselves. From the nature of the case these new unions could not employ the privilege-methods of their skilled superiors—apprenticeship and demarcation rules were out of the question where apprenticeship did not exist and crafts were not defined ; nor, being poor, could they place much reliance on the reserve strength afforded by large friendly benefit funds. The only method which remained for them was to strengthen their own ability to secure an improved price for their labour by substituting a collective bargain on behalf of the whole group of workers in place of the individual bargain of each separate worker with an employer. By bargaining collectively through a trade union they could establish a " standard rate " to arrest the tendency of individual workers to undercut one another by bidding for employment and so cumulatively lowering the supply-price at which labour was offered over the whole trade. As long as some workers stood outside the union and were not included in the collective bargain, the " standard rate " only applied over part of the trade, and the possibility still remained of the standard being undercut by the competition of other workers who offered their labour at a lower rate. It accordingly became the dominating aim of the new unions to make their organization as all-embracing as possible ; their ideal being to prevent the employment of non-union labour altogether ; whereas the employer on his side had a natural interest in reserving the freedom of what in America is called the " open shop " to substitute non-union for union labour if he desired.

At the outset the old craft unions were inclined to look with contempt, if not with actual hostility, on these new unions among the lower grades. But as the new unions grew in strength and influence, while on the other hand industrial development rendered the privilege-methods of the Old Unionism increasingly obsolete, the craft unions were even inclined to look to the younger unions for alliance and support. Where unskilled workers to an increasing extent could encroach on skilled workers' jobs, as in the engineering trades, the power of the craft union on its own to exact terms from an employer was considerably weakened. On the other hand, a strike of unskilled workers could often be easily broken by the employers if the skilled craftsmen (for instance, engine-drivers on the railways) stood apart and continued at work. A certain sense of interdependence accordingly developed between the two sections ; and this prepared the soil for a movement towards Industrial Unionism, or the linking up of all workers in one industry, irrespective of craft or grade, into a single organization, which filled the stage of trade union discussion in the decade before the First World War. The arguments in favour of such reorganization had special force, since in England trade unionism, like Topsy, had " just growed," and the unplanned growth had resulted in a multiplicity of sectional, over-lapping and often rival unions—over 1,000 in all. The need for larger units of organization, to increase the effectiveness of collective bargaining, was sufficiently felt to bear fruit in a number of amalgamations and federations of separate unions. Many of the separate craft unions merged together, as in the engineering trades, where the Amalgamated Engineering Union was eventually formed out of the old Amalgamated Society of Engineers along with several other craft unions. Unskilled workers' unions which overlapped were joined or federated, as in the case of the Transport Workers' Federation. Generally, however, the attempt to link up both skilled and unskilled workers in a single industrial union met with too strong resistance from the skilled crafts, who feared to lose their privileges if merged in a larger unit. The signal achievement of the apostles of industrial unionism was the National Union of Railwaymen, formed in 1913 to include all grades in the railway service; but even here two craft unions, the Associated Society of Locomotive Engineers and Firemen and the Railway Clerks' Association, remained outside.

§ 5. Trade Unions and the State. Collective Bargaining inevitably implied the use of the strike weapon as a last resort if the bargainers failed to come to terms. Just as an individual bargain is not free if one of the parties has not the right to refuse to close on the other's terms, so a collective bargain can have no meaning unless the parties have full right to refuse to close the bargain if they are not satisfied; and this means on the employers' side the right to refuse to employ the workers on the latter's terms, and on the workers' side to refuse to work on the master's terms—in other words, to declare a strike. In the event of such a collective refusal to agree, the master will desire to obtain either non-unionists, or deserters from the union, or workers from another town or trade who will accept employment on his terms. If he can do this, he can " break the strike " : if he cannot, his hope of victory will be confined to a trial of endurance with the union, until the latter's funds are exhausted and starvation forces it to " come to heel ". The strikers on their side will rely for success, not only on the power to hold out and keep themselves from starvation, but also on the ability to prevent the masters from staffing their factories with " blacklegs ". To do this by dissuading non-unionists from entering the factories is the purpose of " picketing "—posting union " pickets " at all entrances to places of work—which plays such a prominent part in every strike. Such " persuasion " may take a variety of forms, from a polite suggestion to a " blackleg " that he should " stand by his mates " to the besieging of a man's house and the use of personal violence. Legislation in 1871 and 1876 had expressly permitted " peaceful picketing " so long as no threats, either in word or gesture, were used ; [1] and it had also removed the illegality which had previously attached to strikes as conspiracies " in restraint of trade ". But in 1901 an important legal judgment, known as the Taff Vale case, laid trade unions open to the danger of being sued as corporately responsible for any acts committed by its members during a strike—if a striker broke a window the national union could be held responsible—and also of being sued for damages on account of losses incurred by employers as the result of a strike. This situation caused the new unions and even some of the older craft unions to join in forming the Labour Representation Committee (later to become the Labour Party), and to run independent candidates for Parliament, in order to secure legal sanction for the right of collective bargaining and the strike. This their pressure was successful in doing ; and in 1906 the Liberal Government passed the Trades Disputes Act by which the Taff Vale judgment was explicitly reversed.

[1] The 1927 Act attempted to narrow the definition of " peaceful picketing " by forbidding expressly the " watching and besetting " of a man's house, the attendance of pickets in such numbers or in such a manner as to " intimidate " anyone ; " intimidation " being defined as causing " apprehension of boycott, or exposure to hatred, ridicule or contempt ". This Act has always been regarded with hostility by the trade unions, and after the Second World War it was repealed by the new Labour Government.

Once having entered politics to secure legal recognition for their activities, it was natural that the trade unions should seek to use political action directly in furtherance of their aims. This led to the policy of securing State interference in the labour market in order to set a " standard rate " by law and thereby raise the supply-price of labour, particularly among the most poorly paid. In other words, it resulted in the policy of the legal minimum wage.

§ 6. Reformist *v.* Revolutionary Trade Unionism. Having passed from bargaining on detailed wage-rates to furthering a general political policy, the New Unionism had come to adopt a definite social philosophy. This social philosophy has come to be known in England as State Socialism : in Continental Socialist circles it is termed Reformism. It involved the acceptance (at any rate for the time being) of the main characteristics and institutions of the wage-system, with the co-existence of a propertied and a propertyless class which the system implied ; but at the same time it involved the attempt to extend State interference in the labour market, both to give legal status to trade unions as recognized institutions of a wage-system, and to raise the standard of life of wage-earners by minimum wage-legislation and allied means. In certain cases it implied also the control or supersession of the private employer by the State.

This view, however, of the correct goal of trade union policy met an important alternative opinion in working-class circles. The alternative was not of very great importance in this country before the First World War, when economic conditions favoured easy improvement in the working-class standard of life ; but it came to be of considerable importance between the wars, particularly on the continent of Europe. This latter policy, usually termed Revolutionary Trade Unionism, regarded it as the function of the trade unions to act as spearheads of a revolt against the wage-system itself, until the working class was sufficiently powerful to challenge the rule of the propertied class and to transfer the control of industry to the workers' own political and economic organizations. This view does not deny the desirability of trade unions struggling by collective bargaining for reforms in the workers' standard of life; but it denies that such attempts should be confined to what is " practicable " or " reasonable " within the wage-system. Every such struggle for reform, it is argued, necessarily comes up against the limits imposed by the rights and desires and standards of consumption of the propertied class : the " practicality " of a wage-advance is relative to what is conventionally accepted as the reasonable standard for the investing class. Hence every claim for advance in Relative Wages is likely to challenge the continuance of these accepted rights and standards, and if pressed by the trade unions these claims are likely to meet increasingly severe resistance all along the line, until the revolutionary issue is finally raised of the very continuance of a propertied class. In certain countries on the Continent this led to the formation of new unions in rivalry to the old Reformist unions ; but in the course of the 1930's there was a tendency towards re-uniting separate unions, and in nearly all cases this was done. With two unimportant exceptions there was no such formation of separate unions in this country ; though under various forms there was an acute struggle between these two tendencies, generally taking the form of " rank and file movements " inside the unions, opposed to the policy of the higher officials and advocating a more militant and " forward " policy.

§ 7. **Workers' Control.** The issue between the divergent views of trade union policy becomes particularly clear when the question of workers' participation in control of industry is raised.

In recent years the matter of admitting wage-earners to some participation in the control of industry has been increasingly discussed both among employers and employed. The crudest form has been the proposals advanced by some employers for what in America are termed " company unions "—associations of work-people belonging to a particular firm—as a means of attaching workers more securely to a particular master, of weakening the hold of trade unionism and substituting individual bargains in place of collective wage-agreements. Sometimes schemes of co-partnership and profit-sharing, such as were described in Chapter III, are introduced, with or without conditions which weaken the attachment of the employees who participate in the scheme to a trade union. In a number of cases the employers, while fully recognizing trade unions and continuing to negotiate with them, have encouraged the formation of elected works committees as a means of increasing loyalty to the firm, of assuaging industrial unrest and increasing the worker's willingness to work and his efficiency. These works committees, elected by the employees in the factory, sometimes are merely instruments for ventilating grievances to the management ; sometimes they have definite advisory functions of passing their opinion on changes and innovations, such as the appointment of foremen, the introduction of new processes, alteration in the shift system ; sometimes they are given a degree of control over specific things such as welfare work, sanitation, or minor matters of time-keeping and discipline. In this country the institution of such councils in each factory was recommended by the Whitley Committee set up by the Government during the First World War ; and up to 1920 about 1,000 were created on the initiative of employers, most of which soon went out of existence. In Germany, between 1920 and 1932, works councils were compulsory by law, and were given certain defined legal powers of a minor order. In the majority of cases the trade unions put forward their own candidates for election to the councils and frequently dominated them ; but in certain cases the employers used the works council " to drive breaches into the principle of collective bargaining ".[1]

The trade unions on their side have advanced claims for some participation in control as a logical development of normal collective bargaining. When a wage-agreement has been made between the employers and a trade union, there frequently remain detailed matters of interpretation in applying the terms of an agreement to the particular case. This will involve such matters as weighing and measuring, which were discussed in Chapter III, the question of hours and overtime, and in the case of skilled workers matters of apprenticeship rules and demarcation of work. When work is on piece-rates difficulties of interpretation are particularly numerous since there is always the question of the category in a " price-list " into which a particular job falls, while the most comprehensive " price-list " can hardly cater for every variation of jobs and certainly not for such new types of work and new processes as may arise. It is inevitable that a trade union, pursuing the aim of collective bargaining, should not be content merely with laying down the general terms of an agreement, but should desire to have some say in the manner of its application to detail. Moreover, the sale of labour has this peculiarity. Unlike other commodities, the seller of labour does not cease to have an interest in what he sells as soon as the act of sale is completed : he has a vital concern in the way in which his labour is used after it has been sold. A wage that might be considered good under normal circumstances may be " low " if the place and manner of employment involve danger to health and life. In some trades working conditions in the factory are already dealt with in collective agreements between employers and trade unions. In textile

[1] C. W. Guillebaud, *The Works Council*, p. 62.

weaving clauses are to be found which provide that workers shall not be required to work where there is an undue volume of steam; and in the potteries that ovenmen shall not be required to work in a temperature higher than 120 degrees. The demand for a voice in the control of working conditions in the factory, as well as over interpretation of piece-work scales, demarcation of work, hours of work and overtime, naturally develops as collective bargaining becomes more complete; and as trade unions grow stronger they inevitably advance claims to have a say in wider matters which affect the workers' interest—on business policy so far as it affects unemployment, on methods of engagement and discharge (e.g. the casual labour problem), even on the general organization of the industry in so far as it affects the ability of the trade to pay good wages.

During the Second World War there came into being in the war industries bodies known as Joint Production Committees, which concerned themselves with the improvement of production in the factory and with organizing the latent initiative of workers towards this end. What was interesting and significant about these bodies was that the initiative in their formation so largely came from trade unionists and in particular from the shop stewards (persons elected by trade union members in each workshop to represent them in any negotiations with the management at the workshop or the factory level). In contrast with the attitude prevailing among militant trade unionists during the First World War, this new development represented, among an important section of trade unionists, a new attitude towards questions of production: a sense that these were no longer the province exclusively of the management and the " higher ups " but the responsibility also of the working class.[1] In October, 1941 a body called

[1] The Report of the International Labour Office on *British Joint Production Machinery* (Studies A, No. 43, 1944) largely attributed the

the Engineering and Allied Trades Shop Stewards' National Council convened an unofficial conference to stimulate interest in the question and to pool experiences. About the same time the main trade union in the engineering trades, the Amalgamated Engineering Union, initiated a series of enquiries into production-questions among its branches, and in February and March of the following year proceeded to negotiate agreements with the Director-General of Ordnance Factories under the Ministry of Supply and with the Engineering and Allied Employers' Federation, whereby every encouragement was to be given to the institution of Joint Production Committees in each factory. These bodies were composed of representatives of the management and representatives elected by the workers in the factory. They were generally separate from the Shop Stewards' Committee or Works Committee, concerned mainly with questions of wages, although the two types of committee often had some of their personnel in common. The total number of these bodies that came into existence during the war is not known. But an enquiry by the A.E.U. in the autumn of 1942, covering nearly 900 firms with a total of a million and a quarter workers, revealed that about 550 of them had joint production committees, of which 88 per cent discussed production-questions in the strict sense of the term (e.g. absenteeism, improved use of labour-force and machine-tool capacity, lay-out of plant, progress, inspection and design, training and dilution) as well as welfare questions; and in March, 1943 a survey made by the Engineering Employers' Federation indicated that 54 per cent of the firms replying considered that such committees had worked wholly satisfactorily, while another 23 per cent reported moderately

incentive towards " the spontaneous movement for production committees in the workshops " to " the entry of the U.S.S.R. into the war " and " the wide publicity given to the part played by the workers throughout the U.S.S.R." (13).

successful results. Pit Production Committees established in
the coal-mining industry had on the whole a less successful
record (no doubt because of the long years of bitter relations
between management and men). After the war, however,
attempts were made to reinvigorate them, following the new
Government's announcement of the forthcoming nationalization and reorganization of the industry ; and the miners'
trade union appointed a special production officer to co-oper-
ate in the Government's campaign for increased coal production. In engineering, however, with the passing of the
special needs imposed by the emergency of war, most of these
committees were disbanded or fell into disuse, despite a post-
war agreement between the trade unions and the employers'
federation to continue the war-time arrangements.

§ 8. The Machinery of Collective Bargaining. The actual
machinery of collective bargaining itself, as it develops, tends
to merge by degrees into machinery which may be described
as an elementary form of workers' control over industrial
policy. At its most elementary and undeveloped stage collective bargaining takes the form of negotiations between an
individual employer and a deputation of his work-people,
without any recognition by the former of the right of a trade
union to speak on behalf of his men. The next stage may
be where a trade union has secured sufficient recognition for
periodic meetings to take place between the officials of the
union and either individual employers or the officials of an
employers' association. Such negotiations here take place as
a rule only when disputed points arise, and only by the
consent of the employers at the moment. A further stage is
reached when the two parties agree to summon a joint meeting
of the two sides at the request of either. Here again meetings
only take place when a dispute has actually arisen ; but the
parties virtually bind themselves to meet and negotiate before

taking any action. Finally, collective bargaining in its most developed form is found when regular machinery is set up in the form of a joint committee of the two sides or a conciliation board composed of representatives of the employers and the trade unions, which holds meetings at regular intervals to discuss current business, and possesses a definite constitution and rules of procedure. As recently as immediately before the First World War in this country important groups of employers, including railway companies, refused to recognize the right of trade unions to bargain for their employees ; and it was only after the advent of the Roosevelt administration that in American industry collective bargaining advanced beyond the most elementary first stage. But in the principal industries in Britain to-day regular machinery exists such as in the fourth stage that we have described, and protracted negotiations take place to arrive at a settlement before the dispute reaches the acute stage of a strike or an employers' lock-out. In some cases the machinery is purely local in character, in others national, covering the whole country ; in many cases both district and national machinery exists ; and trade unions generally favour national negotiation and national agreements, since these give the greatest possibility of establishing a standard rate over the whole industry. In some cases special provision is made for referring the dispute to an impartial arbitrator, if the two sides cannot agree by conciliation. The arbitrator then gives his judgment on the merits of the case, which the parties are free to accept or reject as they choose.

§ 9. **Conciliation and Arbitration.** In Britain the Government has confined itself to encouraging the voluntary institution of conciliation machinery of the above kind. The Conciliation Act of 1896 provided that agreements arrived at by such conciliation boards might be registered, if the parties agreed,

N

and have the force of civil contracts ; and it further empowered the Board of Trade to appoint an arbitrator to give a decision on a dispute on the application of both parties. The Industrial Courts Act of 1919 extended these provisions, instituting a formal Arbitration Court to which disputes might be voluntarily referred, and empowering the Minister of Labour to set up a Court of Enquiry at his discretion to investigate and to publish the facts of any dispute. The Whitley Committee proposed that every industry where organized bodies of employers and workers existed should institute a permanent standing Joint Industrial Council, representing employers and employed, and having regular meetings to discuss current business. There was to be no compulsion in the institution of these : the Ministry of Labour was to " encourage " their formation and to give them every facility, but that was all ; and in the years after the First World War these Whitley Councils, as they came to be called, were instituted in a large number of industries. It was the original intention of the framers of the Report that, starting as mere conciliation boards (such as already existed in the larger industries), they should gradually extend their discussions to wider matters concerning their several industries and become virtually parliaments of industry, with powers of joint control. In practice they have developed little further than conciliation boards which meet regularly and not merely when a dispute has already arisen. Having no powers to deal with matters which the employers do not choose to refer to them, and able only to achieve anything by agreement between the two sides and not by a majority decision, they have been confined in the main to discussing agreements over wages and hours. It had been the intention of the Whitley Committee that at a future date the Government should take action to give legal force to decisions arrived at by Whitley Councils, so that their agreements about wages and working conditions could become

binding upon a whole trade ; and recommendations in this
sense were subsequently made both by the Whitley Council of
the boot and shoe industry and by the Trades Union Congress.
No action was taken to give general effect to this intention.
But, as we shall see in the next chapter, something akin to it
was done in the case of two industries in the 1930's, by making
an agreement arrived at between representative organizations
of employers and workers legally binding on the whole trade
by special order of the Minister of Labour at the request of
the representatives of the industry : an arrangement which
was extended more widely to industry during the Second
World War and for a period of five years after the war.

CHAPTER VIII

THE STATE AND WAGES

§ 1. **State Intervention.** The " standard rate " which a trade union attempts to establish by collective bargaining is in effect a minimum wage. But it is subject to the consent of the employers to the terms of the proposed bargain ; it applies only to those firms that are voluntary parties to the agreement ; and even if registered, as the Conciliation Act of 1896 enables it to be, the agreement has only the force of a civil contract to bind it, affording a possibility to the trade unions, if they care to go to the trouble and expense, of suing employers for arrears of wages where the agreed rate is not paid. When, however, the aid of the State is summoned to institute a *legal* minimum wage, this minimum can be enforced compulsorily over the whole or a particular part of the trade, and it then becomes a criminal offence, punishable in law, for an employer to pay less than this legal rate.

The machinery and method of minimum wage enforcement is varied. First, different minima may be fixed for different industries by *ad hoc* boards appointed to deal with each industry alone. Secondly, a national commission may fix the minima for various industries, using its discretion as to how far to vary the minima in the differing cases. Thirdly, an actual figure may be laid down in an Act of Parliament as a minimum to apply over the whole country. In the first case the minima of different industries may vary quite widely, being fixed on different principles and according to the differing conditions of industries ; and as a result the criterion of relative " fairness " in the wage-level, as it was defined in Chapter VI, may not be observed. In the second case the

180

different minima are likely to approximate much more closely, and to show greater co-ordination. But, on the other hand, the single national body may be less cognisant of the precise conditions in a particular industry than a board specially appointed to deal with that trade. A figure laid down in an Act of Parliament—to take the third case—is likely to be insufficiently flexible and adaptable : it may be at the same time sufficiently high in some industries where low-grade labour is employed to hamper employment, and sufficiently low relatively to existing standards in other industries to have no significance there as a minimum. The first of these methods was that adopted in England under the Trade Board system, and in the Wages Boards which are found in certain Australian States, most notably in Victoria and Tasmania. The second system has existed in certain parts of Canada and U.S.A., and in New South Wales, Queensland, West Australia, and New Zealand. An example of the third method is the Minimum Wage Act of New South Wales of 1908, which prohibited the employment of any person at less than 4s. a day. Similar clauses are to be found in the legislation of Queensland, Victoria, and West and South Australia, New Zealand and a few States of U.S.A.

§ 2. The Wages Council System. The first legislation of this kind in England, the Trade Boards Act of 1909, was intended specifically to deal with the problem of the " sweated trades ". It was, therefore, designed, not so much to raise the general level of wages all round, as to raise the supply-price of labour in cases where it was abnormally low, and to adjust wage-rates in these trades on a principle of " fairness " relatively to what was customarily paid for the same type of work elsewhere. The Act applied by name to four trades—tailoring, paper-box making, machine-made lace and chain-making—and empowered the Board of Trade to institute such machinery (subject to Parliamentary confirmation) where, and only where, it was " satisfied that the rate of wages prevailing in any branch of the trade is exceptionally low as compared with that in other employments ". The characteristic feature of these Boards was that, while (unlike the subsequent Whitley Councils) they were compulsorily constituted, they had mainly a representative character, being predominantly composed of persons chosen as representatives of employers and employed in the industry. The major element of the Board was, therefore, persons who intimately knew the nature of the trade with which they were dealing; and to this extent it was a case of the industry legislating for itself. To represent the standpoint of the State, however, a certain number of " appointed members "—usually economists or prominent social workers, or occasionally lawyers—were added to the Board; and in practice these had considerable influence as a deciding voice between the two sides. It was the duty of the Board to fix a rate which it considered reasonable as a minimum. If it chose, it could appoint sub-Boards for particular districts or sections of the trade, with the duty of making recommendations to the National Board, but without the power of making decisions on their own; and the National Board had the option either of fixing a single minimum for the whole trade, or, on the advice of its sub-Boards, of causing the minimum to vary to suit the different conditions of different districts. The rate or rates on which it decided, subject to confirmation by the Board of Trade, then became the legal minimum for that industry, enforceable in criminal law. By 1913 four other trades had been added to the original four; and by 1918 thirteen Boards were in existence, covering nine trades and half a million workers. The only other instances of minimum wage legislation in England (apart from the special case of the munition trades during the War) were in agriculture and coal-mining. Under the Coal Mines Minimum Wage Act of 1912, which followed the coal strike of that year, district boards in the principal coalfields, composed of employers and workmen with an independent chairman, were empowered to fix minimum rates below which a piece-worker's earnings should not fall. In 1917 the Corn Production Act established a national minimum of 25s. for agriculture. This war-time arrangement was terminated in 1920 ; and after 1924 minima were fixed by District Wages Boards, composed of representatives of farmers and agricultural workers, with the addition of " appointed members " nominated by the Ministry of Agriculture. In both of these cases, therefore, the fixing of rates was in the hands of *district*, and not national, bodies.

During the First World War the Whitley Committee recommended that the functions of Trade Boards should be widened, and that from dealing specifically with sweated trades they should be extended as a substitute for collective bargaining to all unorganized trades where no adequate machinery for collective bargaining existed. This intention was embodied in an amended Trade Boards Act of 1918, which gave power to the Minister of Labour to extend the Act (without specific sanction of Parliament) to any trade where in his opinion " no adequate machinery exists for the effective regulation of wages throughout the trade ". The result was a considerable extension of Trade Boards, until by 1921 they had been instituted in a further 28 trades, and covered some million and a half work-people, of whom nearly three-quarters were women. This virtually represented the high-water-mark of minimum wage action between the Wars. The rapid extension of the system aroused keen complaints from employers as soon as trade depression and a falling price-level appeared in 1921, particular objection being lodged against the habit of many Boards, not only of fixing minima for the lowest-paid workers in each trade, but of fixing separate minima

for the better-grade workers as well. Bowing to these complaints, the Government instituted a Committee of Enquiry
under Viscount Cave ; and this Committee reported in 1922 in
favour of a certain curtailment of the functions of the Boards.
It was suggested that in future the criterion of an " unfairly "
low wage-rate, as adopted by the 1909 Act, should be employed
as well as that of " no adequate machinery ", which the 1918
Act had used as a substitute principle ; it was suggested that
minima for workers other than the lower grades should be
enforceable only by civil action, and not under the criminal
law ; and greater facilities for district boards within an
industry, fixing different district rates, were advocated. No
new legislation was introduced to embody the recommendations of the Cave Committee ; but the Ministry of Labour
announced that for the future its administration of the existing
Act would be guided by these recommendations.

In the early part of the 'thirties the Trade Board system
was extended to two small trades, cutlery and fustian-cutting,
where wages among women workers were found in many
cases to have been very low (half the women time-workers in
cutlery receiving less than 6d. an hour and a quarter of all
women workers in fustian-cutting). Later the system was
extended to the bakery and furniture trades ; and in 1944
the total number of such Boards was 52. The pre-war decade,
however, witnessed two important new developments in
minimum wage legislation, apart from the Trade Board
system. These developments took the form, not of instituting
a statutory board with independent members to lay down a
minimum, but of giving statutory effect to agreements already
arrived at between trade unions and employers' organizations,
and making the agreed rates of wages binding as minima
over the whole of the trade. In 1934 the Cotton Manufacturing Industry Act attempted to deal with the special
problem of low earnings (largely due to under-employment)

in cotton-weaving by making wage-agreements binding as minima; and under the Acts governing road transport in 1932 and 1933 it was provided that certain types of licence to road hauliers should be conditional on the observance of labour conditions at least as good as those laid down by agreement of employers' and workers' representatives through the conciliation board for the road transport industry. The Road Haulage Wages Act of 1938 went further and established a Central Wages Board (with Area Boards), to include a certain number of independent members from outside the industry; the Board to lay down a " statutory remuneration " for all workers employed in connection with vehicles coming within the two main categories of licences. During the War, in 1943, a special Act was passed to introduce legal minimum wages into the catering trades by a special procedure. Under it a Commission was set up to survey the requirements of the situation in the industry, and on its recommendation Wages Boards were to be set up for those sections of the industry where no satisfactory machinery for the voluntary determination of wages existed.

Finally in 1945 a comprehensive Act, entitled the Wages Councils Act, was passed, which, while re-enacting the main provisions of the Trade Boards Acts of 1909 and 1918, re-named Trade Boards as Wages Councils and gave them some additional powers such as the right to determine a guaranteed weekly wage. For the future the Minister of Labour was empowered to establish such a Council where " no adequate machinery exists for the effective regulation " of wages or, on the recommendation of a commission of enquiry, if no adequate voluntary machinery exists whereby wages can be regulated. It was further provided that, for a temporary period of five years after the war, employers in any trade would be under obligation " to observe terms and conditions of employment not less favourable than those established

in the trade or industry in the district by virtue of agreements " between representative organizations of employers and
workers ; thereby continuing into the peace a provision of
war-time regulation of wages. This obligation on employers,
however, unlike the minima established by Wages Councils,
was not to be enforced by inspection, and there were no
penalties for non-compliance.

§ 3. **Minimum Wage Problems.** One of the main problems
which have faced the Trade Boards has been the fixing of
minimum rates for workers on piece-rates and the question
of allowing abnormally slow or inefficient workers to be
employed below the minimum. To fix a minimum for piece-
workers is particularly complicated, owing to the difficulty of
defining the " piece " ; and to legislate for every possible
type of job, and in such a way as to avoid evasion, is almost
impossible. The only alternative is to adopt the device of
fixing an amount per hour as the least that a worker on
piece-work must receive. But what of the particularly " slow "
worker who does not normally earn as much as this minimum
in an hour ? If the employer is forced to pay him this, the
worker may be dismissed. The 1909 Act provided that an
employer should be considered as having observed the law
if the piece-rate in force yielded the minimum earnings per
hour to the " ordinary worker ". But how is the " ordinary
worker " to be defined ? Here again an arbitrary device has
had to be adopted. The assumption is made that a certain
proportion of the workers are " ordinary "—Mr. Cadbury has
said 95 per cent ; the Tailoring Trade Board ventured the
more cautious estimate of 80 per cent. The remainder are
assumed to be abnormally " slow workers " ; and if workers
are regularly earning less than the minimum, the employer
is required to offer proof that these workers are in some
relevant sense abnormally inefficient. There then arises the

further question as to whether this minimum for piece-workers
should not be set at a higher level than for workers employed
on time-rates, seeing that the former usually work at greater
intensity and produce on an average a quarter or a third as
much again as workers employed on time; and after the
1918 Act certain Trade Boards took the option afforded to
them of fixing a separate and higher basic minimum rate
per hour for piece-workers. To deal with " slow workers "
employed on time-rates, it has been the custom of Trade
Boards to issue special " permits " to employers to pay in
these cases below the minimum hourly rates. It is also
customary to issue " learners' certificates " to enable young
persons who are learning the trade to be paid a special wage.
If the Board is too free in the issue of these permits, possibility
is provided of evading the legal minimum; while if it is too
strict, a number of workers less efficient than the normal,
by reason of age or illness or accident, may be discharged
from employment. Similarly with the special rates and the
" learners' certificates " for young persons who are learning
the trade : if these rates are fixed too low, the employer,
attracted by their cheapness, will tend to take on a large
number of young workers and then discharge them later
when these have to be paid at adult rates ; if the rates are
fixed too high, the employer will not find it worth while to
teach persons the trade, and young workers will be unable to
enter the trade.

A second problem is concerned with the question of varying
the minimum between districts or sections of the industry ;
and much controversy has raged on this point. In some
cases the cost of living may differ from one district to another,
so that equal *real* wages will only pertain if *money* wages
differ by an equivalent amount. Again, if labour in different
districts is of different quality, the criterion of " fairness "
is satisfied if the lower-grade labour in one district is paid at

less than the higher-grade labour elsewhere. In such cases a certain variation of the minimum rates between districts may be desirable : otherwise, if the rate is fixed with reference to the high-grade district, it may rob the lower quality workers in the other district of employment ; while if it is fixed at a level which is adequate to the latter district, it may be too low to give any adequate protection to the workers in the former. Similar considerations apply to the fixing of different rates for different grades of workers generally. But where no such differences of quality exist, there is no case for allowing firms in a district to pay lower rates than elsewhere simply on the ground that they " cannot afford " to pay higher— the frequent complaint, for instance, of small dressmaking establishments in the country or of small shopkeepers or of out-of-date collieries. To discriminate in favour of these would simply be to subsidize the inefficient employer and to encourage labour and capital to stay in districts and employ- ments where it was less productive than it might be elsewhere. The only question here is the possibility of moving the surplus labour from the less efficient districts or sections of the trade which cannot stand the imposition of the national minimum, and finding it alternative employment. Only if such move- ment of labour presents considerable difficulty is there a serious case for allowing a permanently lower district minimum in that locality compared to others. In general Trade Boards seem to have favoured the fixing of national minima for the whole trade—too much, indeed, in the opinion of the Cave Committee—and have generally allowed district variation only where special circumstances seemed clearly to demand it.

More difficult than problems of fixing minimum rates has so far been the difficulty of enforcing them. It is a principle which is now fairly well established by experience that a law left for enforcement to the workers' own initiative is almost invariably a dead-letter. The workpeople are probably ignorant of the terms of the law in the first place ; even if they realize that they are being illegally cheated, they are probably too afraid of losing their employment to take action ; while even if this is not so, the workers have seldom the means or the legal experience to engage in prolonged litigation. Where strong trade unions exist, these may make it their business to investigate non-observance of the law and to start legal proceedings ; but the industries covered by Wages Councils are precisely those where trade union organization does not exist or covers only part of the trade. The responsibility for enforcing the minimum rates, therefore, falls on the inspectorate which is maintained by the Ministry of Labour for this purpose. It is to be noted that in the case of workers on piece-rates inspection is apt to meet with special difficulties in detecting breaches of the law. Formerly this inspectorate was quite inadequate for its task : in 1924 it sufficed to visit no more than 3 per cent of the enterprises concerned, at which rate a firm would only be inspected on the average once every thirty years. Since then there has been improvement in this respect. By 1931 the number of inspectors had been increased to 67, and an annual inspection of 25 per cent of the firms subject to the Trade Boards Acts was achieved ; and whereas in 1923 and 1924 the inspectors detected breaches of the law in some 30 per cent of the firms which they visited, by 1931 this percentage had fallen to some 12 per cent of the firms.[1] In the post-war years inspection covered about 10 per cent of the establishments involved.

§ 4. State Arbitration. When the State fixes a minimum wage, it does not fix what the wage must necessarily be—this is left for bargaining to determine, and bargaining may determine a wage above the minimum. All it does is to fix a

[1] Cf. *Report of the Ministry of Labour* for the years 1923 and 1924 and for 1931.

minimum limit below which bargaining is not free to settle on a wage. But in some cases the State goes further, and seeks to supplement or even supplant collective bargaining, by setting up machinery to adjudicate as to what the contractual wage settled between the two parties shall be. In its simpler form this has consisted in making a collective agreement binding on the parties to it, not merely as a civil contract, but in the sense that it becomes a legal offence to refuse to observe the agreement. This may be done either at the discretion of the Government or only in cases where the parties agree to register it and so to endow it with legal force. As a further stage in compulsory action, a collective agreement may be made what is called the " common rule "—that is, made binding over the whole trade, whether party to the original agreement or not. This may also be done either at the discretion of the State (as happens in Queensland), or only at the request of the parties who have signed the original agreement, as was the case in the cotton-weaving industry in England under the 1934 Act, referred to in the last chapter. In a more developed form we find the system as part of a general system of compulsory arbitration, where a Board of Arbitration or an Industrial Court (as in New South Wales, Queensland, New Zealand and South Australia) gives a decision as to what it considers to be a reasonable wage in the trade, and this becomes legally binding on employers and employed alike. Sometimes the arbitration court gives its award only when a dispute has arisen, and the award is applicable only to the parties to the dispute. In other cases the award can be made on the initiative of the court at any time, and can be made the " common rule " for the whole trade. When State interference has reached this stage, the freedom of collective bargaining disappears, and instead the State assumes responsibility for regulating the level of wages. But while the State forbids the workers collectively to refuse

to work at the wage-rate which it lays down, and forbids
employers to challenge the legal rate by a general lock-out
(if that can ever be clearly defined) it cannot, short of much
more sweeping measures, prevent employers from reducing
the employment that they offer if they consider the legal rate
too high.

§ 5. The Future of Wage Policy. In the situation following
the Second World War discussion increasingly centred round
the impact on wage-problems of three novel developments:
the introduction of a comprehensive system of social insurance,
giving security from destitution ; an extension of the sphere
of State control, and in some cases of actual State ownership
and operation of industry ; and the possibility of a greater
approach to conditions of full employment than had before
been achieved in peace-time. If men ceased to be haunted
by want and the unemployed reserve army were to disappear,
the labour market would become, in Sir William Beveridge's
words, " a sellers' market " instead of a " buyers' market "
for the first time (apart from exceptional periods such as a
war). These developments placed two questions on the
agenda of post-war discussion. Firstly, there was the question whether the movement of labour between industries and
localities that would be necessary if the pattern of production
were to be adaptable in face of economic change could be
successfully achieved by means of an appropriate wage-policy,
and whether it was desirable that wage-policy should be
governed with this end in view. Secondly, there was the
question whether the new situation demanded some sort of
centrally co-ordinated wage-policy, worked out between the
Government and the trade unions at a high level, and involving
a substantial modification of the traditional system under
which the level of wages was separately determined in each
industry by the process of autonomous collective bargaining.

The answer to the first of these questions may be very different if it refers to the large-scale movements of labour that are required at periods of rapid transition, such as at the beginning and at the end of a war, and movements of labour required in more normal times, which are likely to be much smaller in extent. In the latter case the amount of movement required each year might be no greater than could be met by a deflection of new entrants into industry towards expanding industries which have a future and a stopping of the intake of young workers by declining industries. A fairly gradual transfer of this kind might be adequately achieved through the system of industrial training, and by subsidies towards the cost of such training, combined with propaganda and advice about employment opportunities through the labour exchange system. At the same time one has to remember that the anticipated decline in the population, if it occurs, and the accompanying change in the age-composition of the population, will tend to reduce the ratio of young entrants into industry to the existing number of workers employed in industry; so that the difference in the labour force in various industries which could be made each year merely by deflecting the flow of young workers from one trade to another would become proportionately less. However, a comparatively small difference of wage-rates and of earnings-opportunities between an industry where the demand for labour was expanding and an industry where the demand for labour was contracting might suffice as an inducement to the requisite amount of movement. There is much to be said for the view that the deliberate creation of wage-differences between occupations as a mechanism of moving labour about is undesirable if it can be avoided. It penalizes workers who have chanced to make their careers in occupations which subsequently turn out to need no further intake of labour, and it creates differences between industries both in earnings

and in the level of costs which appear to conflict with equity
and with reason. The effectiveness of such differences in
stimulating movement may be small if they are expected to
be purely temporary ; while, if they are thought to be more
than temporary, their existence may merely provoke a movement in trade-union circles to level up what are regarded as
unfairly low rates in the lower-paid trades.

However, at times when transfer of labour on a much
larger scale is necessary, as at the end of a war, a mere shift
in the intake of young workers will not suffice ; and the
offer of some inducement to labour to transfer to occupations
where the demand for labour is expanding by raising wages
in these occupations will almost certainly be necessary. The
special problem existing at the end of the Second World War
was that wage-differences between industries were often such
as to obstruct rather than to assist the transfer from war
industries to the peace-time industries where expansion was
most needed. In the war industries both wage-rates and
earnings had been relatively high. Mining and textiles that
were handicapped by shortage of man-power offered little
attraction to new entrants because (largely as a relic of the
depression years between the wars) they were badly-paid
trades. We have mentioned above (in Chapter VI) that in a
state of full employment wages in an arduous and dangerous
trade like mining might have to rise to a level very much
higher, both relatively and absolutely, than had been traditional, if new recruits were to be attracted into the industry.
Clearly, in this situation a radical alteration in the wage-
structure, so as to overcome the handicap which these low-
paid trades suffered was a pre-requisite for achieving the
desired distribution of manpower.

A crucial difficulty in the way of a national wage-policy
(if this is thought of as something that supersedes sectional
collective bargaining) is that in this country there is no central

o

" government " of the trade union world, as in some other
countries, capable of taking binding decisions about wage-
policy. Each trade union is an autonomous body, and the
General Council of the Trades Union Congress plays little
more than a co-ordinating rôle. In the post-war years the
General Council agreed to give support to the Government's
policy of " wage restraint ", alternatively known by its critics
as the " wage-freeze ". But it could not prevent an individual
union from pressing for a wage-advance if it decided to do
so ; and when a majority of the trade union world in the
early 'fifties rejected a standstill on wages, the General
Council's " restraint " agreement with the Government became
quite ineffective. There is the further difficulty that there is
no agreed body of principles as to how labour should share
in the product of industry and in increases of that product,
or even as to the " correct " relationships (or " differentials ")
to be observed between the wages of different kinds of occupation (quite apart from the question we have discussed above
as to whether or not wage-differentials should be used as a
means of " moving labour about " from occupation to occupation and from place to place). At any rate there is little, if
any, sign that trade unions would be willing, in private industry
at least, to give up their rights of independent collective
bargaining over wages—and less that the rank and file trade
union members would agree to do so even if the trade union
officials at the top were willing.

INDEX

ABRAMS, M., 22
Advantages, Principle of Equal
Net, 138–41
Agriculture, 145, 161, 182–3
Allen, Prof. R. G. D., 38
Amalgamated Engineering
Union, 162, 168, 175
America, *see* U.S.A.
Apprentices, Statute of, 164
Apprenticeship, 142, 163–6, 173
Arbitration, 177–9, 189–91
" Aristocracy of Labour ", 157–
158, 161
Associated Society of Loco.
Engineers, 168
Australia, 30, 45, 157–8, 181, 190

BARGAINING-POWER, 97, 99, 107,
118 seq., 160 seq.
Barna, T., 19, 22
Bedaux System, 63–6
Berlin, 37
Beveridge, Sir William, 191
Board of Trade, 36, 45, 178, 182
Bolton List, 80
Bonus Systems, 60–6, 77, 78
Boot and shoe industry, 29, 45,
69, 79–80, 83
Bowden, Witt, 41
Bowley, Dr. A. L., 19–20, 30, 34,
39, 46
Brassey, Lord, 51, 119
Briggs, Henry, Son & Co., 76
Bristol, Survey of, 48
British Medical Association
standard, 47–8
Budgets, 32–8
Builders' Union, 162
Building trade, 46, 146, 161–2,
164

Butty System, 70–1

CADBURY, 186
Cairnes, J. E., 143, 149
Calories, 34–5
Capital :
export of, 19, 157–9
fixed and circulating, 14, 58,
98, 102, 103–4, 112–13, 122
strike of, 127, 137
See also Investment
Capitalism, 19, 22, 97, 126, 135–
137 ; *see also* Wage-System
Casual labour, 28, 146–7
Catering trade, 185
Cave Committee, 184, 188
Charity, 100
Checkweighmen, 73–4
Children, *see* Families *and* Social
Insurance
China, 156, 157, 158
Clark, Colin, 19, 22, 41
Clark, Prof. J. B., 105
Classes, 2–4, 9–11, 17, 96
Clerical workers, 144
Clothing trade, 45, 148, 181
Coal industry, 44, 45, 63, 71, 73,
82–4, 87, 141, 146, 149, 161,
176, 182–3, 193
Collective bargaining, 69–70, 76,
77, 79, 79–80, 107, 118 seq.,
160 seq., 176–7, 189–91,
193–4
Combination Acts, 162
" Common rule ", 190
*Compagnie d'Assurances Géné-
rales*, 76
Competition, 92, 106, 120, 128,
163, 166
imperfect, 128–30, 153–4

Conciliation, 177–9, 180
Consumption, 44 seq., 117, 126–8, 132, 136 ; see also Food
Control, Workers', 171–6
Co-partnership, 76–7, 78, 129
Corn Laws, 99, 156
Cost :
  labour, 50–4, 113–16, 121–3
  of living, 17, 23 seq., 32 seq., 39–43, 81, 83, 131, 155–6
  overhead, 57
  prime, 13, 78–81, 114–15, 131
Cotton industry, 29, 44, 45, 63, 73, 80–1, 149, 156, 161–2, 174, 184, 193
Crafts, 141–4, 162–8
Craftsmen, 3, 4, 5, 10, 11, 161, 164–5
Crusoe, Robinson, 1
Custom, 93 seq.

DECASUALIZATION, 147
Demand, 23, 24, 91, 102 seq., 113–17, 120 seq., 132, 149–151
Dependence, economic, 8
Determinism, 88–9, 98, 107, 133–4
Diet, 33–4, 53 ; see Food
Differential Piece-rate System, 58, 62
Dilution, 70, 167
" Diminishing Returns ", 105
Disraeli, B., 13
Distribution of income, 17, 22–3
Dockers, 28, 73, 147, 166
Domestic System, 10–11, 71
Douglas, Prof. Paul, 54, (and Jennisson), 21
Dunlop, J. T., 21, 26

EARNINGS, 16–17, 27–32, 40–4, 45–9, 77–81

" Economy of High Wages," 51–2, 101
Education, 140
Edward I, King, 3
Efficiency, 41, 51–4, 121, 122, 151–3, 155, 156, 158
Elasticity of demand, 103, 115–116, 120–1, 126, 132
Elasticity of supply, 54, 108, 109, 110–11, 153
Emerson system, 62
Employers, 7–9, 12–13, 14
  self-employer, 3–4
Employment, see Unemployment, Demand
Employment Exchanges, 130
Enclosures, 9–10
Engineering industry, 29, 43, 46, 69–70, 162, 167–8, 175
" Equal Pay for Equal Work ", 154–5
Equality, see Inequality, Advantages
Excess Capacity, 130–1, 132, 135
Exploitation, 2–4, 7–14, 54, 59, 70–1, 72–3, 74, 128–30, 131, 147–9, 153

" FAIRNESS ", of wages, 142, 144–6, 154, 156, 187
Family, 27, 30–1, 44–9
Family allowances, 49
Federation of Cotton Spinners, 162
Flint Glassmakers, 163, 164
Florence, Prof. P. Sargent, 153
Food, 32–9, 51, 91–3
Ford, Henry, 6, 67
Fox, Head & Co., 76
France, 76, 157
Freedom, economic, 5–9 ; see also Laissez-faire
Frescobaldi, 3
Full Employment, 191, 193

GANTT system, 62
Germany, 3, 9, 10, 22, 37, 157, 172
Gilds, 10, 143, 160, 163
Grades, 29, 42–4, 70, 138–44 ; see Upgrading, Skilled, etc.
Grand National Consolidated Trades Union, 162
Guillebaud, C. W., 173

HABIT, 93 seq.
Halsey, F. A., 61
Hart, P. E., 19–20
Henderson, Prof. Sir H. D., 119–120
Hepburn, Thomas, 161
Hicks, Prof. J. R., 120
Hosiery trade, 73, 83
Hours of Work, 54, 85–7, 124, 173–4
Huddersfield Weaving List, 81
" Human Needs Standard ", 44–5, 48

IMMIGRATION, 156–7
Imperialism, 157–8
Incentive, 54 seq.
Income :
    distribution, 17, 19–23
    national, 19–23, 135–6
    workers', 16–27, 53–5, 74–5, 133–7, 193–4
Index numbers, 32 seq., 42, 84
India, 156, 157, 158
Industrial Courts Act, 178
Industrial Reserve Army, 97 ; see also Reserve, Unemployment
Industrial Unionism, 167–8, 172–5
Inequality, 5–9, 17, 140–6, 155–9
Inflation, 23–5, 40
Intensity of work, 27, 41–2, 55 seq., 110

Interest, rate of, 114, 137
International Labour Office, 36–37, 174–5
Inventions, see Machinery
Investment, 102, 108–9, 116–17, 126–8, 132
Ireland, 52, 163
Iron industry, 73

JEVONS, W. S., 105, 119, 120, 124
Joint Production Committees, 174–6

KALEČKI, M, 20, 115
Keynes, Lord, 26
King, Dr., 20
Knowles, K. G. J. C., 43
Kuznets, Dr. S., 20

LABOUR :
    aristocracy of, 157–8, 161
    casual, 28, 146–7
    cost, 50–4, 78–81, 113–16, 121–3
    Government, 169, 176
    intensity, 27, 41–2, 55 seq., 110
    market, 9–10, 125–6, 128, 131, 132, 134, 138 seq., 191
    Party, 169
    productivity, 41, 50–1, 105–6, 121, 131, 156–8, 194
    supply of, 8–14, 54, 58, 91 seq., 110 seq., 125, 129, 141 seq., 150–1, 153
    turnover, 13, 58, 129
    See also Ministry of L., International L. Office, Wages, Trade Unions
Laissez-faire, 118 seq.
Lavers, Commander G. R., 48
Law, economic, 19, 88–90, 92–3, 106, 133–4
" iron l. ", 96
Learners, 187 ; see also Apprenticeship

" Leaving certificates ", 130
Legislation :
  factory, 72–4
  hours, 87
  industrial relations, 177–9
  trade union, 162, 169–70
  See also Truck, Social Insurance, Wages Councils
Leicester, 80
Lewis, E. L., 142
Lithographic Printers, 164
Liverpool, 47–8
London, 37
  Survey of, 47
Long period, see Short period

McCulloch, J. R., 71–2
Machinery, 18, 80–1, 97, 112 seq., 121, 136, 164–5
Malthus, T. R., 92, 97, 98, 101
Marcet, Mrs., 14, 99–100
Marginal Productivity, 103 seq., 123, 151–2
Marginal Utility, 104
  of income, 7, 111, 125
Market :
  buyers', 18, 191
  labour, 9–10, 125–6, 128, 131, 132, 134, 138 seq., 191
Marshall, A., 91, 102, 103, 106, 107–9, 125
Marx, K., 96 seq., 102, 112–14
Merseyside Survey, 47–8
Middle Class, see Professional workers
Mill, J. S., 95, 98, 99, 119, 120, 129
Minimum, see Wages
Mining, see Coal
Ministry of Labour, 30, 32, 35, 37, 45, 83, 178, 179, 183, 185, 189
Mobility of labour, 102, 129, 130, 138 seq., 148, 156–7, 191–4

Monopoly, 13, 19, 21, 24, 115, 129, 130–3, 136, 137
" Mutuality ", 69

National Income, see Income
National Industrial Conference Board, 64
National Union of Railwaymen, 168
Nationalization, 171, 176, 191; see also Socialism
Necessaries, conventional, 93 ; see also Diet, Poverty, Food
Net Advantages, Principle of Equal, see Advantages
Net output and income, 13–15, 21
" New Deal ", 21, 177
" New Unionism ", 165–8
Nicholson, J. L., 42
" Non-competing groups ", 7, 141–4, 149, 151, 156, 163
North Lancashire List, 81
Northampton, 79
Northcott, Dr. C. H., 64
Norwich, 80

" Old Unionism ", 162–5
Oldham List, 80
Output per worker, 41 ; see also Productivity
Overtime, 28, 30, 42, 70, 86, 173, 174
Owen, Robert, 162

Pareto, V., 22
Payment by Results ; see Piecework, Bonus Systems
Peasants, 3, 9–10
" Period of Production ", 58
Phelps Brown, Prof. E. H., 19–20
Piecework, 29–30, 55 seq., 152, 173, 174, 186, 187, 189

Pigou, Prof. A. C., 20, 41, 43
Pit Production Committees, 176
Point-rating, 63–6
Poor Law, 100
Population, 31, 46, 92, 94–5, 97, 98, 99, 101, 192
Postgate, R. W., 161
Poverty, 44 seq., 101, 125, 151
Powell, J. E., 68
Premium-Bonus Systems, 60 seq., 78
Priestman System, 61–2
Printing Industry, 46, 155
Productivity of labour, 41–2, 50–4, 105–6, 120–1, 131, 156–8, 194
Professional workers, 142–4
Profit, 13–15, 20, 57–8, 59, 63, 71, 83–4, 97, 112–13, 114, 120
Profit-sharing, 75–7, 83–4, 129
Proletariat, 5–8, 9–15, 160 seq.

RAILWAY Clerks' Association, 168
Railways, 44, 52, 71, 83, 167, 168
Reformist Trade Unionism, 170–1
Rent, economic, 140
Reserve, of labour, 9–11, 18, 97, 147
Revolutionary Trade Unionism, 170–1
Ricardo, D., 91, 93–8, 114
Richardson, Prof. J. H., 150
Road transport, 185
Robbins, Prof. Lionel, 119
Robertson, D. J., 43
Robertson, Prof. Sir Dennis H., 20, 114
Robinson, Mrs. Joan, 117
Roosevelt, President, 21, 177
Rostas, Dr. L., 22

Rowan, David, 60–1
Rowe, J. W. F., 121
Rowntree, Seebohm, 31, 44–9
Russia, 3, 9 ; see also U.S.S.R.

SALARIES, 22, 141–4
Scandinavia, 34, 36–7
Scotland, 82
Seers, Dudley, 23
Senior, N., 95, 101
Serfdom, 3, 4
" Sheltered trades ", 42–4, 145–6
Shift system, 57
Shipbuilding, 43, 46
Shop Assistants, 20, 87
Shop Closing Acts, 87
Shop Club Act, 75
" Shop Statements ", 79
Shop Stewards, 70, 174–5
Short period, and long, 94–5, 102, 115–17, 122, 133
Skilled workers, 43–4, 70, 138–144, 161–8 ; see also Crafts
Slavery, 2–3, 4, 91
Sliding-scales, 81–5
Slumps, 26, 40
Smith, Adam, 56, 91, 129, 138–140
Social insurance, 49, 191
Socialism, 67, 128, 135, 170
South Metropolitan Gas Company, 76
Southampton, 48
" Speed-up ", 55 seq., 67–8
Standard of life, 30, 33 seq., 52–54, 96–7, 126–8, 136
Standardization, 29
State :
    and wages, 178, 181–94
    property, 17
    See also Wages, minimum ; Legislation, Nationalization
Static theory, 95, 98, 133
Stockholm, 36–7

Strikes, 76, 167, 168–9, 190–1;
    see also Capital
Sub-contracting, 70–2
Subsistence Theory, 91 seq., 134
Substitution, 101–2, 103–5, 112–
    117, 120–3, 136–7, 151–2
Supply and demand, 91, 96, 107
    seq., 163
Supply-prices, 54–5, 108–9, 110–
    111, 125, 145, 150–4, 159
Surplus, 2–4, 13–15
    capacity, *see* Excess Capacity
    of labour, *see* Reserve
Sweated trades, 124, 147–9
Sweden, 36–7

TAFF Vale judgment, 169
Tailoring, *see* Clothing trade
Taussig, Prof. F. W., 142–3
Taxation, and income-distribu-
    tion, 22–3
Taylor System, 62–3
Teachers, 142, 144, 149
Textiles, *see* Cotton
" Tied cottages ", 13
" Time and motion " studies,
    59
" Time-preference ", 108
Time-rates, 67–70, 72, 79–81,
    152
" Tommy-shops ", 13
Trade Boards, 46, 181–9; *see
    also* Wages Councils
Trade cycle, 19, 26, 40
Trade Unions, 12, 19, 67, 69, 71,
    72, 76, 77, 96–7, 99, 107,
    118 seq., 146, 153, 154, 160–
    179
Trades Disputes Act, 169
Trades Union Congress, 64, 179,
    194
" Treasury Index ", 42
Truck, 74–5

UNEMPLOYMENT, 13, 27–8, 40–1,
    46, 47, 48, 90, 115–17, 120,
    121, 147, 191
" Unsheltered trades ", 43–4
Unskilled workers, 43, 70, 138–
    144, 165–8
Upgrading, 29, 30, 42
U.S.A., 6, 13, 20–2, 45, 54, 60,
    61, 62, 64, 122, 157, 158,
    159, 177
U.S.S.R., 67, 130, 175

VARIATION, Principle of, 122

WAGES :
    absolute, 16
    bill, 16
    Councils, 32, 46, 181–9
    differentials, 43, 138 seq.,
        191–4
    earnings, 16–17, 27 seq., 40–4,
        45–7
    Fund, 98 seq., 109, 113
    minimum, 32, 118, 121, 178,
        180–91
    payment of, 54 seq.
    policy, 191–4
    rates, 17, 27 seq., 55 seq.,
        77–81
    real w., 17, 23 seq., 30 seq., 39
        seq., 84, 131, 136, 155, 187
    relative, 16–17, 18–23, 157
    system, 1–15
    theory of, 18–21, 23–6, 50–4,
        88–159
    See also Piecework, Bonus
        Systems, Trade Unions
Wales, 82, 146
Wartime, 40, 42, 69, 86, 130,
    174–6, 183
Washington Conference, 87
Webb, Sidney and Beatrice, 123,
    152, 163
" Weights ", 34, 37, 38–9

Weir, Halsey-W. System, 61
Whitley Committee, 172, 178, 183
Whitley Councils, 178–9
Women's wages, 54, 149–54, 184

" Work Fund ", 56
Works Councils, 70, 172–3, 175–6

YORK, 44, 49